THE

COLLECTION

Celebration and Vision:

The Hewitt Collection of

African-American Art

Todd D. Smith

Catalogue design by RLR Associates, Inc.
Indianapolis, Indiana

Contents

Preface

There are moments in the cultural life of a city that truly demonstrate the value of the arts to all people. The arrival of *Celebration and Vision: The Hewitt Collection of African-American Art* is one of those moments. The fifty-eight works of art in this collection are but a small part of a rich and varied personal collection of art, history, culture, and memories. Assembled over fifty years, the Hewitt Collection not only includes masterpieces of twentieth-century African-American art, but also in its totality offers a survey of African-American art and society.

The Hewitt Collection above all is a testament to the building of communities. For John and Vivian Hewitt, this community took the form of an extensive network of friends and artists, many of whose works are represented in the collection. The stories the Hewitts tell of trips to studios and countless parties—or "salons" as Vivian loves to call them—give us insight into the lives and careers of a constantly evolving group of African-Americans. Further, the personal notes inscribed on many of the works in the collection, which were written on special occasions in the life of the collectors, stand as a lasting honor to the shared lives of the collectors and the artists.

For Charlotte, *Celebration and Vision: The Hewitt Collection of African-American Art* offers another opportunity for building community. This project has become a citywide event. Purchased as a gift for the Afro-American Cultural Center and set to premiere at the Bank of America Gallery at the new Mint Museum of Craft + Design, the exhibition, the accompanying catalogue, and the educational programming have brought people together from all of Charlotte. The result is an event that celebrates the cultural life of Charlotte and betokens a bright future for continued collaboration across the arts and other disciplines.

At Bank of America, we take this as very good news. Like our predecessor institution, NationsBank, Bank of America is founded on the conviction that our company is only as strong or as healthy as the communities where we do business. We are extremely pleased to present this exhibition to our neighbors in Charlotte as well as communities across the country as it travels over the next three years.

I encourage all who see the exhibition to reflect on the communities of which they are a part, and to think about how the visual world—and visual art—is part of these communities and a cause for celebration.

Hugh McColl, Jr.
Chairman and CEO,
Bank of America

Introduction

Celebration and Vision: The Hewitt Collection of African-American Art represents a coming together of a wide range of voices and expressions regarding African-American culture. "African diasporal culture" is meant as an all encompassing term that affords a gathering place for cultural and social interaction, discussion, and even conflict.

The exhibition catalogue depends upon this concept of a large communal gathering place. To mirror the collection and to emphasize the many who have brought this project to fruition, this catalogue offers something for everyone. In the era of cultural pluralism, such attempts often result in ideas reduced to the lowest common denominator. We offer instead a collection of thoughts that approach the collection from various perspectives and agendas.

We have envisioned this catalogue as a primer for the study of African-American art while simultaneously offering advanced thinking on the nature of race and representation within American culture. The title, *Celebration and Vision*, directs us away from a consideration of the artworks as markers of racial oppression. John and Vivian Hewitt assembled this collection due to both an appreciation of the particular experiences they knew best and out of a love of the visual. Although the collection is not meant to rectify historical injustices, both its very existence and its future role as a public resource offers such a revision. Above all, the collection celebrates expression and passion. Individually the works stand as testaments to perseverance and commitment. As a group the works acknowl-

edge the power of the visual within the lives of not only African-Americans but also the human race.

An explanation of my role in this project might illuminate the scope of involvement across institutions. As curator of American art at the Mint Museum, it is my responsibility to assist Bank of America in programming its gallery which is a part of the new Mint Museum of Craft + Design. Out of early discussions for the inaugural exhibition for the gallery, we decided to present an exhibition of African-American art from the bank's collection. At about the same time, the bank became aware of the availability of the Hewitt Collection. Once the bank decided to purchase the collection as a gift to the Afro-American Cultural Center, it was natural to place the exhibition in the new Bank of America Gallery. The bank has chosen to support both the publication of this catalogue and the national tour of the exhibition. At press time, the exhibition is scheduled to appear in Washington, D.C., Jacksonville, Atlanta, Memphis, Los Angeles, St. Louis, and Dallas.

I have many to thank. I must first thank the officers of Bank of America, formerly NationsBank. The singular vision and drive of Laura Foxx of the Bank of America Foundation has brought the collection to Charlotte and to the rest of the country. I remember the first morning Ms. Foxx and I met at the Hewitt's home to review the collection. I was immediately struck by her astute observations about the art and her passion for the magnificent possibilities the collection held for Charlotte. Her spirit has guided this project through many twists and turns, but never has she swerved from the course. I am indebted to her commitment and beneficence. Also, at the foundation, I must make special mention of Tracy Boyce. As director of communications, Ms. Boyce has been instrumental in securing the necessary public exposure for this exhibition. Moreover, Ms. Boyce's humor has relieved many a tense and overwhelming moment. This project's successful completion is due in no small part to Ms. Boyce and her wonderful spirit. Three other individuals, Lynn Drury and Paula Fraher of Bank of America Foundation and Kathryn Blanchard of Crown Communications, have assisted in various aspects of this project, especially public relations and educational opportunities. And finally, but not least, I must extend a heartfelt thank you to both Hugh McColl, Jr., Chairman and CEO of Bank of America, and Marc Oken, Executive Vice President and Principal Financial Executive. Their combined vision and commitment to the arts in Charlotte has transformed the city into a center for the arts. Their belief in this project only serves to confirm their status as cultural brokers of the best kind.

I must extend many thanks to the staff at the Mint Museum of Art. For the Mint to be a part of such a special project reflects well on the vision and commitment to cooperation of the museum staff and board of trustees. I must thank a few specific people who have supported my involvement with this exhibition from the start: Bruce Evans, CEO and President; Charles Mo, director of exhibitions and programs; Kurt Warnke, head of installation and design; Kari Hayes DeLapp, assistant curator; and Diane Curry, curatorial assistant. I have had the assistance of several wonderful volunteers and interns: Courtney Burt, Sharel Brown, and Catherine Smith.

At the Afro-American Cultural Center, director Cynthia Schaal has been essential in bringing this project to fruition. Her commitment to the cultural heritage of both African-Americans and Charlotte has set the standard for our project. Likewise, Stephanie McKissick and Melinda McVaden have provided perspective and assistance throughout the planning stage of this project.

The beauty of this catalogue is due to Rodney Reid of RLR Associates in Indianapolis. Mr. Reid and his firm have handled with assurance and aplomb the problems of working both with such a large group of decision-makers and under tight deadlines. Never did Mr. Reid lose sight of the final product and his commitment to perfection is noteworthy. David Ramsey's photography is another source of great pride for this project. For the condition and the presentation of the collection, I must thank Mark

Boyd and his team at Art Aspects in Charlotte who carefully rematted and reframed most of the pieces in the exhibition.

On a personal level, I must thank the research staffs at the Amistad Research Center and the Schomburg Center for Research in Black Culture at the New York Public Library. Of course, a special debt is owed to the contributors to this catalogue. Culled from all over the United States, these writers have risen to the challenge of such a daunting task and have done so with professionalism and good spirit. A special thanks is to be extended to Kristin Fedders who as copy editor for the entire project has once again proven herself an astute reader and cherished colleague.

A final and special note of appreciation must be given to John and Vivian Hewitt. From our first meeting, this couple has made me feel part of the family and part of their community of artists and supporters. Upon each visit to their home, they further opened their minds and their hearts to me. (They were even so kind as to let a few of us crash John's recent birthday party to acquire footage for a video.) Such dedication to the art and culture of this century is indeed a cause for celebration.

Todd D. Smith
Curator of American Art
The Mint Museum of Art

Celebration and Vision:

The Hewitt Collection of African-American Art

Essays

Understanding Celebration and Vision

Todd D. Smith

Twentieth century black subjectivity is, first and foremost, a choice that, while frequently influenced by the artist's personal identity, is not solely dependent upon it. [1]

-Richard Powell

Perhaps it is too much to hope for a future in which we can recognize differences without seizing them as levers in a struggle for power. However, making this future must involve us all...and white people cannot declare themselves indifferent to racial politics. [2]

-Russell Ferguson

I. Understanding the Terms

Saturated with vibrant color, Jonathan Green's *Easter* adorns the cover of this catalogue; its companion image on the back is a formal portrait of John and Vivian Hewitt, the namesakes of this collection. A deliberate choice, this juxtaposition brackets the essential issues raised by this exhibition and this essay.

Green's painting focuses on the ritual of celebration, in this case the Christian holiday dedicated to Christ's ascension, and provides an appropriate visual metaphor for half of the exhibition's title, *celebration*. The figures are static, to be sure; they are seated and hieratic. The tenderness indicated by the woman's hand resting on her partner's right thigh is offset by the sharpness of their angular forms. The monumentality of the figures' presence is belied by the work's physical size, a mere 11-1/4 x 7-1/2 inches. The painting looms larger than its dimensions would suggest.

If the artist has captured these two figures during an Easter service, the calmness and quietude of the image underscores the solemnity of the occasion. The dignity and stasis might be a simple reflection of the nature of the event. Yet, in its stillness and sternness, the image breaks with the stereotypical view of African-Americans at church. Green's work embodies a different vision than that of African-American women standing in the aisles, shouting hallelujah, and waving paper fans to relieve the heat of both religious passion and the southern clime. The stability of the couple and their commitment to the service offer another mode of celebration.

Easter not only suggests celebration, but also *vision*, the other half of the exhibition's title. On the one hand, the faceless couple is, to use the vernacular, a vision of loveliness and of love. Likewise, Green presents the couple, arrayed in their finery, as a spectacle for the audience's enjoyment. However, although the pair directly confronts the viewer through the forceful frontal orientation of their heads, they are faceless, lacking the external marker of vision. This absence or loss alludes to the powerlessness of blacks within white society, or does it? Cornel West has written that

> the modern Black diaspora problematic of invisibility and namelessness can be understood as the condition of *relative lack* of Black power to represent themselves to themselves and others as complex human beings, and thereby to contest the bombardment of negative, degrading stereotypes put forward by White supremacist ideologies. [3]

To suggest, then, that Jonathan Green suffers from internalized racial hatred seems to be a pat rationalization for the couple's lack of vision. Rather the faceless couple raises the issue of visibility and invisibility within black aesthetic discourse and offers a point of departure for the following review of the collection.

Much has been made over the notion of invisibility within black communities. From Ralph Ellison's classic text *The Invisible Man* (1947) to Marlon Riggs' film *Tongues Untied* (1989), artists and writers have repeatedly drawn upon the gap between visibility and invisibility. Following similar binary strategies, such as center/margin, good/bad, and white/black, the trope of visible/invisible requires not only that each term be discrete, but also that the terms be separate but not equal. Russell Ferguson wrote in his introduction to *Out There* about the issue of center and margin and the inherent assumptions that underpin the operations of these terms: "When we say marginal, we must always ask, marginal to what? Nevertheless, this question is difficult to answer. The place from which power is exercised is often a hidden place."[4] Ferguson seems to turn the tables, for he poses that "we are thus returned to the invisibility of the center." How can the center—the privileged term—be invisible, the secondary term? Ferguson rightly proposes that "in our society dominant discourse tries never to speak its own name. Its authority is based on absence."[5] As such, the facile association of visibility with power and invisibility with service proves problematic. Jonathan Green's emphasis on both visibility and invisibility illustrates Ferguson's assertion of the mutability of the "eithers" and the "ors."

Linked inextricably to the discussion of visibility and invisibility is the centrality of the visual to African-American history and life. Most critics and students have focused their attention on the prominent role of music within the lives of African-Americans believing that the visual plays a less significant role. According to Michele Wallace,

> How one is seen (as black) and, therefore, what one sees (in a white world) is always already crucial to one's existence as an African-American. The very markers that reveal you to the rest of the world, your dark skin and your kinky/curly hair are visual. However, *not being seen* by those who don't want to see you because they are racist, what Ralph Ellison called "invisibility," often leads racists to the interpretation that *you are unable* to see. This has meant, among other things, that African-Americans have not produced (because they've been prevented from doing so by intra-racial pain and outside intervention) a tradition in the visual arts as vital and compelling to other Americans as the African-American tradition in music.[6]

While Wallace does address the importance of vision to the lived experiences of African-Americans, her conclusion begs a more expansive definition of the visual arts. Offering another perspective, bell hooks states:

> Black folks may not identify with art due to an absence of representation. Many of us do not know that black folks create diverse art, and we may not see them doing it, especially if we live in working-class or under-class households…the point is that most black folks do not believe that the presence of art in our lives is essential to our collective well-being…black folks have tended to see art as completely unimportant in the struggle for survival.[7]

Missing from this assessment is a deeper understanding of the role of vision within African-American culture. Vision—arguably more than music and performance—has been key to the establishment of black identity. If we consider for a moment the physical ability to see as a part of the concept of vision, we will understand better the point at hand.

Within our society, race is signified not by genetic difference but by appearance. The body is the location of difference. Black skin equals a black person, white skin a white person. Although such a reduction is admittedly simplistic, this reduction underscores how our society determines race. In modest terms, the ability to *read* race relies on the ability to *see* race. The instances of misinterpretation of race based on insufficient visual details are legendary. The entire phenomenon of passing hinges on visual acuity. Douglas Sirk's remake of *Imitation of Life* (1950) offers a superb example of the high stakes of passing. Starring Lana Turner as Lora Meredith and Juanita Moore as Annie Johnson, this maternal melodrama, which concerns the failures of mothers and daughters to develop relationships that can sustain societal expectations, is in fact driven by passing. Rehearsing a litany of the problems between mothers and daughters (and equally concerned with Turner's off-screen domestic rollercoaster), the film ultimately concerns race and vision because Annie's daughter, Sarah Jane, attempts to pass as white. In the pivotal scene, Annie travels to the West to find her daughter who is a dancer at a dance club, the Moulin

Rouge. Annie sees her daughter passing as white amidst a cast of white dancers. When Annie meets Sarah Jane in the dressing room after the performance, Sarah Jane misunderstands Annie's motives. Although Annie has come to offer her support, the daughter is convinced that she has come to take her back to Connecticut. Annie cries, "I only wanted to look at you," equating looking with affirmation. In the course of the dialogue Sarah Jane responds, "I just wanted to be white." These two admissions of desire demonstrate how looking intersects both racial identity and passing.

Upon her return home, Annie dies of a broken heart. As she takes her last breaths, the director underscores the conflation of passing with sight. A photograph of Sarah Jane, walking the line between genetic racial identity and represented racial identity, separates Lora (Turner) on the left and Annie (Moore) on the right. The climactic scene emphasizes the price of passing. As Annie's casket is slid into the hearse, a wailing Sarah Jane emerges from the crowd and throws herself at the casket, exclaiming, "I didn't mean it. I'm sorry mama...I killed my mama." While in the final scene Lora both hugs Sarah Jane and reaches out to her own daughter, Susie, in an attempt to reconstitute the family, the gesture fails. Passing transcends cinematic closure and thus demonstrates how race is always concerned with representation. As Stuart Hall has remarked,

> We tend to privilege experience itself, as if black life is lived experience outside of representation. There is no escape from the politics of representation, and we cannot wield "how life really is out there" as a kind of test against which the political rightness or wrongness of a particular cultural strategy or text can be measured.[8]

Many historians of African-American art have spent time compiling basic biographical data and commenting on the lack of information. Richard Powell has suggested a new strategy:

> African-American art history (which has long been restrained—and shrouded—by the requirements of a biographical and strict chronological approach) takes on a new character that, rather than being intellectually bound by the perceived race or nationality of a creator,

looks instead to the art object itself, its multiple worlds of meaning, and its place in the social production of black identities.[9]

With Powell's strategy in mind, Green's *Easter* becomes not an illustration of black invisibility and powerlessness, but an iconic presence emblematic of the need to rethink vision and race in American culture. Accordingly, this exhibition considers the acquisition, presentation, and maintenance of this incredible collection of art, culture, and memories, rather than revisiting the history of oppression within the visual arts. We rejoice in the accomplishments of the Hewitts, the artists they befriended and collected, and the opportunity to keep the collection intact. The juxtaposition of their photographic portrait with Green's painting celebrates their vision.

II. Building a Collection and a Community

When Bank of America first asked me to assess the Hewitt Collection, the poignant and plentiful inscriptions that embellish the margins of many artworks reminded me of the relationships that the Hewitts shared with the artists. In many ways, these annotations rival the imagery for dominance, underscoring the importance of both margin and center. As written texts accompanying visual texts, these personal salutations insert into the collection the community around the collectors. However, I want to make clear that this idea of community does not derive from a stereotypical conception of a "black community," implying a static and universal group. Rather, the idea of a localized and particular community served as the impetus to build the collection.

From their adolescent and early adult years, John and Vivian Hewitt have shown an interest in the visual. For John, the interest manifested itself in the simple act of clipping illustrations from *Life*—including images by artists such as Pablo Picasso—and placing them on his bedroom wall. For Vivian, a reproduction of François Millet's *The Gleaners* on the wall in her aunt's home spurred her interest in art. Likewise, she remembers vividly a schoolbook reproduction of a Rosa Bonheur painting. While such memories may not be uncommon, they indicate the enduring centrality of the visual to the couple.

The couple met in Atlanta on 17 September 1949. John began teaching at Morehouse College in 1948 and Atlanta University hired Vivian to work in the library in 1949. They spent their honeymoon in New York City immersing themselves in art and used the nuptial cash to buy prints from museum stores. The Hewitts bought their first original work from Vivian's cousin, J. Eugene Grigsby. Ever the entrepreneur, Grigsby had sold $10 shares in his artistic ability to family members, and the Hewitts augmented this support by purchasing one of Grigsby's works in the early 1960s. While the designation "the first artwork by an African-American to be collected by the Hewitts" is significant, the friendship that grew between the artist and the couple demands closer attention.

While Grigsby was in graduate school at New York University, completing a doctorate in art education under Hale Woodruff, he introduced the Hewitts to the black cultural elite in New York City. Stories abound about their introduction to various artists, dealers, and other collectors, such as when Vivian and John followed Grigsby to Romare Bearden's home so that Grigsby could photograph some images. This first encounter, like so many to follow, led to a blossoming friendship and an increasing level of support. Grigsby also introduced the couple to Charles Alston and Norman Lewis.

Adele Glasgow, John's sister, also introduced her brother and sister-in-law to the black cultural elite. Glasgow, along with her partner, ran the Market Place Gallery in Harlem, which served as a salon from 1959 to the early 1960s. In March 1959 at the opening of their inaugural exhibition, *10 Contemporary Artists*, Langston Hughes read from *The Weary Blues* to the music of Randy Weston, Jimmie Corbath, and Charles Rousse. As the personal assistant, researcher, and confidante to Langston Hughes from 1952 to 1962, Glasgow knew many artists and writers. In 1949 Jacob Lawrence was commissioned to execute twelve illustrations for Langston Hughes'

fig. 1

John Hewitt & Hale Woodruff (right)
at Woodruff show
photo by Vivian Hewitt
May 1980

book of poems, *One Way Ticket*. Of these, only six were used in the publication. In 1979 Glasgow gave the Hewitts one of the unused images which Hughes had willed to her. Hughes and Glasgow also introduced Vivian to Elizabeth Catlett whom she met in Mexico City in 1958. This was one of nine meetings between the Hewitts and Catlett. Through Glasgow, the couple also met Ernest Crichlow, Earl Hill, Hughie Lee-Smith, and Margaret Burroughs.

By 1978 the Hewitts were firmly entrenched in the art world of black New York. One evening, while entertaining Alvin Hollingsworth in their home, he proposed that the Hewitts exhibit his work at their home. Such a request stunned John and Vivian, who had been committed to purchasing, not selling, art. Nevertheless, Hollingsworth prevailed and this tentative foray into sales proved propitious for the Hewitts. While never charging a fee from the artists, these gallery presentations often provided the couple with immediate access to works by artists whom they admired. In fact, at the first show for Hollingsworth, the Hewitts purchased all of the works by the

fig. 2

Charles Alston (1907-1977)
Woman Washing Clothes, ca. 1970
oil pastel on paper
The Hewitt Collection

artist currently in the collection. Future exhibitions included shows of works by Woodruff (fig. 1), Crichlow, and Grigsby.

III. Toward a Broader Appreciation

Most historians of African-American art either have addressed the stereotypical representation of blacks or have rehabilitated artists whose careers have been overlooked. As bell hooks writes, "many folks think the problem of black identification with art is simply the problem of underrepresentation…"[10] She continues that

> representation is a crucial location of struggle for any exploited and oppressed people asserting subjectivity and decolonization of the mind…the question of identifying with art goes beyond the issue of representation. Our capacity to value art is severely corrupted and perverted by a politics of the visual that suggests we must limit our responses to the narrow confines of a debate over good versus bad images.[11]

In an extended exploration of this debate, Kobena Mercer has explored both the reflectionist and the social engineering arguments. Cornel West has summarized Mercer's views:

> The reflectionist argument holds that the fight for Black representation and recognition must reflect or mirror the real Black community, not simply the negative and depressing representations of it. The social engineering argument claims that since any form of representation is constructed—i.e., selective in light of broader aims—Black representation (especially given the difficulty of Blacks gaining access to positions of power to produce any Black imagery) should offer positive images of themselves in order to inspire achievement among young Black people, thereby countering racist stereotypes.[12]

As these authors and others have suggested, this paradigm limits understanding to the notion that African-American artists have been overlooked, neglected, and co-opted.

For me, the Hewitt Collection, the history of its formation, and its new role as a public trust requires a different paradigm for understanding the racial identity of these artists. This collection defies a simple definition of African-American art and reinvests the term *diversity* with pluralism and possibility. The eventual repository for the collection, the Afro-American Cultural Center in Charlotte, demands that we consider this collection as more than an assemblage of great works of art. Instead, I would like to focus on the collection as a group of images of black popular culture. The placement of the collection within the context of a cultural center spurs this consideration because I think it prompts a reconsideration of the role of the visual within the black experience. This approach takes nothing away from the masterpieces within the collection and encourages a new understanding of African-American art that accounts for the intersection of great art and popular imagery.

For a cultural center with specific goals such as the Afro-American Cultural Center, images are needed to tell a story, to demonstrate technique, to provide communal focus, and to engender enjoyment. For a cultural center (as opposed to an art museum), these images must engage the popular realm. If regarded as simply works of great aesthetic value, their use is only partially realized. The works in the Hewitt Collection are visual texts that belong to an expansive grouping of visual imagery concerned with local and universal experiences. This might be used as a counter to the comment made by bell hooks' sister that as blacks "we can identify with movies and we don't feel we know how to identify with art."[13] For the Hewitt Collection to remain vital and vibrant, it must be allowed to operate across the spectrum of visual realms. It must continue to challenge the split between high art and popular culture, asserting its identity as both and neither.

Stuart Hall has suggested that

> in one sense, popular culture always has its base in the experiences, pleasures, memories, traditions of the people. It has connections with local hopes and local aspirations, local tragedies and local scenarios that are the everyday practices and the everyday experiences of ordinary folks.[14]

We only have to reflect on the Hewitt's description of Charles Alston's *Woman Washing Clothes* (fig. 2) to understand the personal appeal of the image. John says that when he first saw the work at an opening at the Manhattan East Gallery it reminded him of attending one of Vivian's family reunions in North Carolina. He recalls how a similar tub was filled with oil for a fish fry. Vivian constructs a different context for the image: she remembers her mother making apple butter in similar pots. Although the image of woman slaving over a tub may anger some viewers, the collectors treasure the image's ability to conjure pleasant memories. Thus, the artworks evoke both the personal and the universal. Ultimately, the oscillation between these two poles generates the significance of the Hewitt Collection and defies any attempt to define the collection in terms of simplistic binary oppositions. Hall has said:

> By definition, black popular culture is a contradictory space. It is a site of strategic contestation. But it can never be simplified or explained in terms of the simple binary oppositions that are still habitually used to map it out: high and low; resistance versus incorporation; authentic versus inauthentic; experiential versus formal; opposition versus homogenization.[15]

If we reconsider the instability of visible/invisible, we find that the Hewitt Collection encompasses this contradictory space. Within different contexts and for different audiences, the collection fosters images and ideas about identity within twentieth-century American culture. Finally, my epigraphs suggest that a discussion of the visual must acknowledge not only that representation prompts an interpretation of race, but also that race cannot be reduced to appearances.

Cultural Identity in African-American Art, 1900-1950

Regenia Perry

Throughout the history of art produced by Americans of African origin in the United States, there has been a conscious effort among many of the artists to create works reflecting an African heritage as well as the African-American experience. In some instances, the same artists worked simultaneously in mainstream styles. The earliest examples of African-American art belong to the category of handicraft, including slave-made artifacts produced primarily in the Deep South during the years prior to the Civil War. The persistence of African motifs in African-American minor arts, and in some examples of folk art, is evident and continues to exist. The advent of official or academic African-American art did not occur until the mid-nineteenth century. By that time, the cultural link with Africa had been diffused and the professional African-American artist produced art that reflected the mainstream art world in which the artist sought acceptance. The background for the first half of twentieth-century African-American art was provided by the careers of the three most accomplished, turn-of-the-century African-American artists: Robert S. Duncanson, Edward M. Bannister, and Henry O. Tanner. Although there were other outstanding contemporaneous African-American artists, their works are not as well-known. Nineteenth century academic African-American artists realized early on that they were facing both racial and professional discrimination, and in almost every instance sought cultural exposure. A better understanding of the issues surrounding African-American art may be ascertained from a brief review of major art movements and related events during this early period.

Robert S. Duncanson was the earliest widely acclaimed African-American artist. Born in Seneca County, New York, to a Scottish-Canadian father and an African-American mother, Duncanson moved to Cincinnati, Ohio, during his youth, where he affiliated himself with both the local artists and the abolitionists, and emerged as one of the leading members of the midwestern school of romantic landscape painters. Duncanson made many trips to Europe, financed by his father and by local abolitionists. He visited England, France, Scotland, Italy, and perhaps Germany, where he made numerous sketches that later became the subjects of his paintings. In addition to landscapes, Duncanson painted portraits, still lifes, murals, and historical subjects.

Edward M. Bannister's desire to become an artist was fueled largely by an article he read in the *New York Herald* in 1867 that stated, "The Negro seems to have an appreciation for art while being manifestly unable to produce it." Bannister moved to Boston, Massachusetts, in 1848 from St. Andrews, New Brunswick, Canada, where he was born in 1828. His father was a native of Barbados in the West Indies and his mother's racial identity is unknown. Shortly after arriving in Boston, Bannister learned to make solar prints and began painting. He was the only major African-American artist of the nineteenth century who developed his talents without the benefit of European travel or study. In 1871 Bannister moved from Boston to Providence, Rhode Island, and painted there until his death in 1901. Shortly after arriving in Providence, Bannister established himself as a landscape painter and community leader. Remarkably, within five years after settling in Providence, Bannister was accomplished enough to submit *Under the Oaks* to the Philadelphia Centennial Exposition of 1876 where it was awarded a medal. Subsequently, Bannister noted that the judges had become indignant when they discovered the artist's race and wanted to reconsider the award. The white competitors upheld the decision, the artist received the award, and a private collector purchased the painting for $1,500. While the majority of his paintings are landscapes, he also pro-

fig. 1

Henry O. Tanner (1859-1937)
Gate in Tangiers, ca. 1910
oil on canvas
The Hewitt Collection

duced portraits, figural studies, religious scenes, marines, still lifes, and genre scenes.

The most celebrated turn-of-the-century African-American artist was Henry Ossawa Tanner (fig. 1). Born in Pittsburgh, Pennsylvania, he moved to Philadelphia, Pennsylvania, as a young boy and lived near Fairmount Park where he frequently observed artists painting and sketching. Tanner was inspired to become an artist as well, much to the disappointment of his Methodist bishop and his family who had hoped that he would become a minister. Tanner drew and painted constantly throughout his teens and after overcoming family resistance enrolled in the Pennsylvania Academy of the Fine Arts in 1880. He studied with Thomas Eakins who exerted significant influence on his early style. In 1888 Tanner left the Pennsylvania

Academy before graduating and moved to Atlanta, Georgia, to join one of his brothers, a minister. Although he established a modest photography studio and hoped to earn a living by selling drawings, making portraits, and teaching art classes at Clark College, his efforts were unsuccessful.

In 1888 he sold his gallery in Atlanta and moved to Highlands, North Carolina, a small resort town in the Blue Ridge Mountains near the Georgia border. Tanner thought that Highlands would be good for his health and that he could earn a living by taking pictures. He rented a small log cabin in the mountains and humorously referred to that summer as his "cornmeal and water regime." Although that business venture was also unsuccessful, he befriended, photographed, and sketched local African-Americans. Those images later became the basis for his early African-American genre scenes.

Tanner returned to Atlanta in 1888 and taught drawing at Clark College for two years. During his second Atlanta sojourn, Tanner met his first patron, Bishop Joseph Crane Hartzell, a member of the college's board of trustees. When Tanner expressed a desire to travel to Europe, the bishop and his wife organized the artist's first individual exhibition in Cincinnati, Ohio, during the fall of 1890. When none of the paintings sold, the Hartzells purchased the entire collection, thereby providing funds for Tanner's first trip abroad. In January 1891 Tanner sailed to Europe. Tanner was so impressed with Parisian art and culture that he decided to remain and abandoned his plans to study in Rome. Tanner enrolled in the Académie Julien where he studied under Benjamin Constant and Jean Paul Laurens. Around 1895 he made the decision to specialize in religious subjects such as *Daniel in the Lion's Den*, which won an honorable mention in the Salon in 1895. Two years later the French government purchased *The Resurrection of Lazarus*, which had won a third-class medal. In 1908 Tanner mounted his first individual exhibition of religious paintings in the United States at the American Art Galleries in New York. In 1923 he was made chevalier de la Légion d'honneur, France's highest honor. He became the first African-American to become a full academician of the National Academy of Design in 1927.

"A dozen years after the founding of the European population at Jamestown, there came another bark from another continent with a human cargo of another color and clime," stated Kelly Miller in an address marking the official opening of the Negro Building at the Jamestown Tercentenary Exposition on 4 July 1907. The exposition celebrated the 300th anniversary of the arrival of the first settlers at Jamestown and provided the first national showcase for African-American achievements. W. Sidney Pittman, an African-American architect who had graduated from the Drexel Institute in Philadelphia in 1900, designed the building, which housed exhibits from African-American public schools. It also featured fourteen dioramas illustrating African-American history from their landing at Jamestown to the first decade of the twentieth century sculpted by Meta Vaux Warrick Fuller. The African-American exhibits placed greater emphasis on industrial arts such as cabinetmaking and carpentry than on fine arts. Indeed, with the exception of Fuller and Thomas Watson Hunster, a landscape painter from Washington, D. C., no major African-American artists exhibited at the Jamestown fair.

The two most influential exhibitions in the United States during the first quarter of the twentieth century—the Eight and the Armory Show—exerted little influence upon African-American artists of that generation. The Armory Show introduced a resistant American public to the latest artistic trends in European painting, including fauvism, expressionism, and cubism. African-American artists joined the crowds who flocked to view the Armory Show. More than a decade after the Armory Show artists such as Aaron Douglas, Hale Woodruff, James Wells, Archibald Motley, and Malvin Gray Johnson began to incorporate cubism into their works.

Although Harlem was named by the Dutch who colonized Manhattan, the name has been associated with black culture since the opening years of this century. Harlem has been described as a city within a city, and many still consider it the greatest African-American city in the United States. Occupying approximately twenty-five square blocks, Harlem reputedly contains more African-Americans per square mile than any other place in the United States. African-Americans have always lived in New York, however, not until the late 1890s did they move northward to West 53rd Street, beginning their migration to Harlem. Three new well-appointed hotels became centers of fashionable life. The Marshall, for example, was a favorite gathering place for actors, musicians, writers, and dancers. Here the first modern jazz band in New York was organized. Called the Memphis Students, this orchestra included banjos, saxophones, clarinets, and trap drums. Florence Mills, Louis Armstrong, Bessie Smith, Leadbelly, and other great musicians achieved fame in the Harlem nightclubs of the twenties and thirties.

The Harlem Renaissance, the Negro Renaissance, or the New Negro Movement, as it was variously called, arose from that vibrant community. The Harlem Renaissance began around 1920 and was the first cultural movement established by African-Americans in the United States. Race consciousness, group awareness, and shared common goals distinguished the New Negroes of the Harlem Renaissance from their peers. Participants focused upon the African heritage of African-Americans. In addition, the National Association for the Advancement of Colored People (NAACP) was founded in 1909 in order to secure civil rights for African-Americans. The Urban League, founded in 1910, helped recent African-American migrants adapt to urban life. Marcus A. Garvey led the ill-fated Back-to-Africa Movement of the United Negro Improvement Association (UNIA). His crusade included a plan to transport large groups of African-Americans to Africa to found settlements. He organized a large corps of uniformed soldiers in his African Legion. Considered the father of Pan-Africanism in America, Garvey played an important role in instilling pride in African-Americans. Primarily a literary movement, the renaissance established a number of African-American artists including Richmond Barthé, Aaron

fig. 2

*James Van Der Zee
A family photo.* ca. 1925
vintage albumen print
collection of Dr. Regenia Perry

Douglas, Meta Vaux Warrick Fuller, Palmer Hayden, Archibald Motley, Augusta Savage, James Wells, and Edwin A. Harleston. African-American publications such as *The Crises*, *Survey Graphics*, *Opportunity*, and *The Messenger* disseminated to a national audience the graphic art of artists such as John Henry Adams, Marcellus Hawkins, Laura Wheeler Waring, and Hilda Wilkerson.

James Van Der Zee, the photographer who maintained a studio in the heart of Harlem for more than fifty years, documented the Harlem Renaissance (fig. 2). Van Der Zee photographed the majority of the African-American celebrities who either lived in New York or traveled there. His GGG Studio located at 272 Lenox Avenue was only a few doors from the corner of 125th and Lenox, Harlem's epicenter. Both the convenient location and his repu-

tation as a master photographer stimulated an increasing stream of customers. Bridal parties went to Van Der Zee's studio following wedding ceremonies and posed among palms, lush foliage, flowers, and a variety of complimentary backdrops. His careful attention to the bridal gowns produced a virtual catalogue of contemporary bridal fashions. Funeral pictures were also popular, and Van Der Zee photographed the funerals of such notables as Florence Mills and Blanche Powell. "James Van Der Zee—Artist and Photographer" was his slogan, demonstrating that he considered himself an artist first. Self-taught, he was both unaware of technological advancements and unacquainted with prominent photographers such as Alfred Stieglitz, Edward Steichen, and Lewis Hine.

In 1922 William Elmer Harmon founded the Harmon Foundation in order to encourage individual growth. The Harmon Foundation announced its Awards for Distinguished Achievements among Negroes in *Opportunity* in 1926, and the foundation sponsored the first major African-American art exhibition in America at the International House in New York in January 1928. Among the most notable exhibitors were Aaron Douglas, Augusta Savage, Sargent Johnson, Palmer Hayden, Malvin Gray Johnson, James A. Porter, William E. Scott, Laura Wheeler Waring, and Hale Woodruff. The foundation's activities included New York exhibitions, traveling exhibitions and the promotion of art education in African-American schools and colleges. By 1933 Harmon exhibitions had traveled to fifty cities in twenty-seven states with attendance exceeding 350,000 (fig. 3). Public response to the Harmon shows varied, and most critics complained about the lack of racial identity and originality in the artworks and the artists' willingness to imitate European styles. One of the harshest critics was Romare Bearden, who emerged decades later as a leading African-American artist of his generation. In an article in *Opportunity* in December 1934, he wrote:

> At present it seems that by a slow study of rules and formulas the
> Negro artist is attempting to do something with his intellect, which
> he has not felt emotionally. In consequence he has given us poor
> echoes of the work of white artists—and nothing of himself.

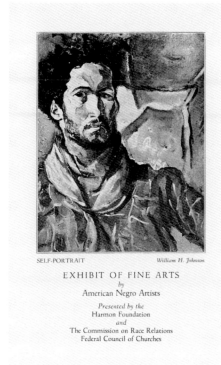

SELF-PORTRAIT   William H. Johnson

EXHIBIT OF FINE ARTS
by
American Negro Artists
Presented by the
Harmon Foundation
and
The Commission on Race Relations
Federal Council of Churches

fig. 3

Cover for *Exhibit of Fine Arts
by American Negro Artists*, 1930
Self-Portrait on cover
by William H. Johnson.
Photograph courtesy
the Hewitt Archival Papers

Despite adverse criticism, the foundation's efforts enabled African-American artists to reach the public.

The Harlem Renaissance prompted many African-American artists to engage their African cultural and artistic heritage. Many artists and intellectuals, including Countee Cullen and Alain Locke, traveled to Paris, as well as to Haiti and Cuba. The first African-American artist to incorporate African forms in his paintings was Aaron Douglas. When Douglas arrived in New York in 1925, the Harlem Renaissance was well under way. During the same year, Locke contacted Winold Reiss concerning the illustrations for his publication *The New Negro*, and Reiss agreed to illustrate the book in

collaboration with Douglas. The book contains three portraits by Reiss and twelve drawings by Douglas. In 1929 Douglas received his first major commission and won national acclaim for his mural designs for the Fisk University Library in Nashville, Tennessee. These murals trace the development of African-Americans from Africa to contemporary America. He later designed murals for the Hotel Sherman in Chicago, Illinois, Bennett College Library in Greensboro, North Carolina, the Countee Cullen Branch of the New York Public Library, and the Harlem YMCA.

Hale A. Woodruff also made his reputation in the 1920s. From 1920 to 1923 Woodruff attended the John Herron Institute in Indianapolis, Indiana. Woodruff first received public recognition when one of his paintings, *Streetworkers*, was accepted in the 1923 Annual Indiana Artists Exhibition. Woodruff also won the Harmon Foundation's painting award in 1926. Using his award money and an additional gift from a patron, Woodruff went to Paris in 1927 where he remained for three years in order to study independently and at the Académie Moderne. While in Paris and southern France, Woodruff completed many landscape and genre paintings, the latter with black subjects. While residing in France, Woodruff and Locke scoured Paris looking for African art. Woodruff returned to the United States in 1931 and began teaching art at Atlanta University.

The reputation of Archibald J. Motley rests primarily upon both portraits and images of African-American nightlife. Born in New Orleans, Louisiana, he moved to Chicago during his early childhood. After graduating from the Art Institute of Chicago in 1918, Motley established a studio in his home and began to paint scenes of African-American life in Chicago. On 25 February 1928 he became the first African-American painter to have an individual show in a downtown gallery in New York. The *New York Times* praised Motley's paintings in a front-page article and included several reproductions in its magazine section. Some reviews were unfavorable: a critic for the *New Yorker* declared that the paintings were too "racial." Motley had been born in Louisiana where memories of slavery were vivid and had developed a spiritual affinity for Africa at an early age. His paintings were fanciful group scenes of how he envisioned life in Africa. At Motley's individual show at the New Gallery in New York, six of his paintings represented scenes from an East African tribe in Uganda worshipping their gods. The African period in Motley's early style stimulated awareness of Africana among the public as well as fulfilling an emotional need for the artist.

William H. Johnson, an avid traveler, journeyed to the American South, New York, France, Germany, Norway, Denmark, and North Africa. During his twenty-one-year odyssey, Johnson absorbed the customs and lifestyles of the various countries and completed hundreds of images in many media. Born in Florence, South Carolina, he recalled copying cartoons from local newspapers during his childhood. He moved to New York in 1921 and attended the National Academy of Design where he won a number of prizes. After living and working abroad, Johnson returned to New York in 1938 where he continued to work and exhibit. The death of his wife in 1943 was a shock from which Johnson never fully recovered, and he continued to exhibit her works in his shows after her death. During the early 1940s, the war provided subjects for Johnson's narrative paintings. In 1944 Johnson visited his mother in Florence and painted a number of portraits of family members and friends. In 1945 Johnson began his final paintings.

During the 1930s, three members of the art department faculty at Howard University—James A. Porter, James L. Wells, and Lois Mailou Jones—joined the steady stream of African-American artists who went to Paris. During the summer of 1935 Porter made his first trip abroad. Through a fellowship from the Institute of International Education, he studied medieval archaeology at the Sorbonne in Paris. With an additional grant from the Rockefeller Foundation, Porter traveled to Germany, Belgium, Holland, and Italy to study collections of African art. In 1945 Porter received the General Education Board Foreign Fellowship to study art in Cuba and Haiti. He spent a year in the Caribbean on leave from his position as chairman of the art department at Howard University. During that trip he completed a

number of Haitian and Cuban scenes and collected photographs and documentary materials.

Noted for painting, lithography, etching, and wood engraving, James L. Wells was born in Atlanta. Following his high school graduation, he attended Columbia University and the National Academy of Design. In 1929 he joined the faculty of the art department at Howard University as an instructor in illustration and later became chairman of the printmaking department, where he remained until his retirement in the late 1960s. In 1921 he participated in the group exhibition sponsored by the Harlem Library, which was the earliest collection of works by African-American artists to be exhibited in New York. Wells affiliated with the Harmon Foundation shortly after its inception and received the Harmon Award in Fine Arts in 1930. In 1933 Wells was appointed director of the Harlem Art Workshop and Studio under the auspices of the Harmon Foundation and the Harlem Adult Education Committee.

Lois Mailou Jones, the only female African-American artist of her generation who enjoyed a consistently successful career, credited both her mother and her teachers with fostering her early artistic interests. She received a scholarship to attend the School of the Museum of Fine Arts, Boston, graduating in 1927 with a teacher's certificate. Jones taught at Palmer Memorial Institute, a private African-American boarding school in Sedalia, North Carolina. After two years in North Carolina, she joined the art faculty at Howard University, where she taught for forty-seven years until her retirement in 1977.

Ten years following her graduation from the School of the Museum of Fine Arts, Boston, Jones received the General Education Board Foreign Fellowship to study in France. She went to Paris in 1937 where she studied painting at the Académie Julien. France provided her with her first feeling of absolute freedom, and her admiration for that country and its people was so profound that she returned to Paris each year for more than twenty years.

Many of the leading African-American sculptors of the turn-of-the-century were female including Meta Vaux Warrick Fuller, Nancy Elizabeth Prophet, May Howard Jackson, Augusta Savage, and Selma Burke. In 1898 Fuller graduated from the Pennsylvania School of Industrial Art. She traveled to Paris in 1899 where she attended the Académie Colarossi and the École des Beaux-Arts. A studio fire in 1910 destroyed most of Fuller's works from her Parisian period. In Paris, she earned the epithet the "Sculptor of Horrors" due to her gruesome subject matter. She exhibited *The Wretched* at the 1903 Salon where it attracted the attention of Auguste Rodin, who accepted her as his student. Following her return to the United States, she married Solomon Fuller in 1909.

Nancy Elizabeth Prophet graduated from the Rhode Island School of Design in 1918. In 1922 she went to Paris where she attended the École des Beaux-Arts and exhibited in the Salon. Prophet developed friendships with Henry O. Tanner, Countee Cullen, and W. E. B. Du Bois. Upon Tanner's recommendation, Prophet submitted two sculptures to the 1930 Harmon exhibition and won a prize for *Head of a Negro*. In 1934 Prophet joined the faculty at Spelman College in Atlanta. In 1944 she returned to Providence.

Augusta Savage's minister-father strongly discouraged her early interest in art. In 1921 she moved to New York and completed a four-year sculpture program in two years. Having received fellowships from the Julius Rosenwald Foundation and the Carnegie Foundation, she studied in Paris. Following her return to New York in 1931 she opened the Savage School of Arts and Crafts and began her career as a teacher. She directed the Harlem Community Art Center, resigning when she received a commission for the 1939 New York World's Fair for which she produced *The Harp* (*Lift Every Voice and Sing*). In the 1940s Savage began to live a reclusive life in upstate New York.

Ironically, the Depression offered opportunities to American artists. In 1933 Franklin D. Roosevelt established the Works Progress Administration, (WPA), which provided jobs for artists. African-American artists, including Aaron Douglas, Hale Woodruff, Charles Alston, and Archibald J. Motley, won numerous commissions to decorate libraries, hospitals, banks, post offices, schools, and other public buildings. WPA projects also included easel paintings. The Index of American Design, another project, employed artists to catalogue American decorative arts, while another group catalogued silver, furniture, and other arts for the Library of Congress. Community art centers, classes, and workshops provided artistic training for many African-Americans.

During the 1940s Romare Bearden, Elizabeth Catlett, Charles White, and Jacob Lawrence emerged as key African-American artists. While Romare Bearden was born in Charlotte, North Carolina, his parents moved to New York when he was an infant. He spent his childhood and adolescent years traveling between New York and the home of his maternal grandmother in Pittsburgh. When Bearden enrolled in New York University in the early 1930s, he had not considered art as a profession and he graduated in 1935 with a degree in mathematics. Bearden's decision to become a professional artist was probably motivated by his association with an informal group of African-American artists in Harlem, the so-called 306 Group, named after the studio lofts at 306 West 141st Street where the group met. During the same year, Bearden enrolled at the Art Students League, where he studied under George Grosz. After eighteen months, Bearden left the Art Students League and painted part-time while working as a social worker. Most of Bearden's paintings of the mid-1940s resemble medieval stained glass windows or synthetic cubism. The year 1940 was pivotal: he met Stuart Davis, who influenced Bearden's later work, and he held his first individual exhibition at the studio of Ad Bates in Harlem. In 1945 he mounted his first individual exhibition at the Samuel M. Kotsu Gallery. The same year the Museum of Modern Art purchased *He is Arisen*. By the early 1970s Bearden was recognized as the foremost American collagist (fig. 4).

fig. 4

Romare Bearden (1912-1988)
Morning Ritual, 1986
collage with acrylic on plywood
The Hewitt Collection

Jacob Lawrence is perhaps the most acclaimed African-American artist of the twentieth century. His paintings have consistently portrayed the lives and struggles of African-Americans and have broad appeal due to their abstract colorful style and universality of subject matter. Born in Atlantic City, New Jersey, he lived briefly in Philadelphia before moving to Harlem when he was twelve. He attended both public school and the Utopia Children's Center, a settlement house that provided afterschool programs in arts and crafts. At that time the center was operated by Charles Alston, who immediately recognized Lawrence's talent. Lawrence enjoyed playing pool at the Harlem YMCA where he met Charles Seifert, self-styled lecturer and historian who had assembled a large library of African and African-American literature. Seifert encouraged Lawrence to visit the Schomburg Library in Harlem, to read everything he could about African-American

culture, and to visit the exhibition of African art held at the Museum of Modern Art in 1935. Under Seifert's influence, Lawrence became interested in the life of Toussaint L'Ouverture, the Haitian independence leader. Lawrence felt that a single painting could not depict the leader's many achievements; thus he produced a series of paintings. The forty-one panels of the *Toussaint L'Ouverture* series were completed in 1938 when Lawrence was twenty-one years old.

Lawrence completed most of his series during the thirties and forties. In November 1941 Lawrence's *Migration* series was exhibited at the Downtown Gallery in New York. The acclaimed exhibition made Lawrence the first African-American to be represented by a mainstream gallery. During that same month *Fortune* published a lengthy article about Lawrence and illustrated twenty-six of the sixty panels. Young, gifted, nonmilitant, and personable, Lawrence embodied the white mainstream ideal of the successful black artist. Overwhelmed by his success, Lawrence was deeply concerned that some of his equally talented African-American artist-friends had not achieved similar acclaim.

Charles White and Elizabeth Catlett also developed careers during the thirties and forties. White's parents had migrated from Mississippi to a black neighborhood in Chicago where he was born. His mother's fondness for reading significantly influenced his early life. His home contained the best books that the family could afford and he frequently visited the neighborhood library. During that period White discovered *The New Negro* (1925) by Alain Locke and learned for the first time the important contributions of blacks to the development of America. During high school his art teachers constantly encouraged him, and by November 1937 some of his work was included in a group show at the Paragon Studio on Michigan Avenue. During the late thirties White secured a job with the WPA in Chicago. The position allowed a number of independent projects and White decided to design a mural titled *Five Great American Negroes*. The mural depicted Harriet Tubman, Booker T. Washington, Marion Anderson, George

fig. 5

Elizabeth Catlett (1917-)

Head of a Woman, 1967

lithograph

The Hewitt Collection

Washington Carver, and Frederick Douglass and was exhibited in Chicago
in October 1939 at the Artists and Models Ball. The mural was later
shipped to the Tuskegee Institute.

In 1941 White married Elizabeth Catlett, a talented sculptor from
Washington, D.C. Catlett has devoted her entire artistic career to a socially
conscious art that conveys black dignity and documents the struggle of
African-Americans (fig. 5). Her sculptures and prints are well-known in
the United States and Mexico where she has worked for many years as
director of the sculpture department at Mexico's National University. She
studied in the art department at Howard University where she graduated
with honors in 1936. She pursued her graduate studies at the University of
Iowa and became the first individual to complete the requirements for the
university's M.F.A. When the chairman of the art department realized that
the department's highest degree would be awarded to an African-American

woman, he contrived to have the same degree conferred upon Catlett's professor. During the same year she received her first prize in sculpture at the
American Negro Exposition in Chicago.

Shortly after White and Catlett were married, White was awarded a fellowship from the Rosenwald Foundation in order to create a mural depicting
the role of blacks in the development of America. In order to study mural
painting, he enrolled at the Art Students League under Harry Sternberg. In
February 1943 White and Catlett left New York for the Hampton Institute
(now Hampton University). There he spent nine months completing
Contributions of the American Negro to Democracy. The artist selected
Hampton Institute as the location for the mural because of the school's
progressive educational programs. In 1946 White and Catlett went to
Mexico City where they attended the School of Painting and Sculpture and
became members of the Popular Graphic Workshop. The couple divorced
in 1947. White returned to New York and had his first individual show in
September 1947 at the American Contemporary Artists Gallery.

The activities of Hale Woodruff during the thirties and forties were important to the evolution of African-American art in the South. Following his
artistic studies in Indianapolis, Chicago, and Paris, Woodruff became
chairman of the art department at Atlanta University. During the summer
of 1936 Woodruff went to Mexico where he studied mural painting with
Diego Rivera. One of the first commissions to demonstrate that influence
was a series of murals that Woodruff painted in the foyer of the new Savery
Library at Talladega College. Woodruff was commissioned to paint the
Amistad murals one century after the 1839 mutiny on the *Amistad*. The
murals established Woodruff's reputation as a muralist. Woodruff was also
involved in a set of panels for the Golden State Life Insurance Building in
Los Angeles, California. In 1949 to decorate the company's new building,
Golden State commissioned Charles Alston and Woodruff to paint two large
murals depicting contributions of African-Americans to that state's history. The panels were unveiled in August 1949 at the dedication services of

the new building and are the most complete representation of African-American contributions to an individual state.

During his sixteen years as chairman of the art department at Atlanta University, Woodruff was responsible for that department's designation as the École des Beaux-Arts of the black South. He organized an annual exhibition for African-American artists that began in 1942 and continued until 1970. During that period, a collection of over 350 works was amassed through purchase prizes. The Atlanta University collection remains one of the largest and most impressive assemblages of African-American art of the twentieth century in a public collection.

In addition to his role as chairman and his reputation as a talented muralist, Woodruff also excelled as a watercolorist and graphic artist. During the 1940s he completed a series of watercolors and block prints. In the 21 September 1942 issue of *Time*, Woodruff stated, "We are interested in expressing the South as a field, as a territory, its peculiar run-down landscape, its social and economic problems, the Negro people." Because most of Woodruff's students came from communities without modern plumbing, Woodruff referred to his group as the "Outhouse School."

The two most outstanding students to emerge from Woodruff's school were Wilmer Jennings and Frederick Flemister. Jennings was born in Atlanta in 1910, earned a B.S. from Morehouse College, and studied with Woodruff for three years. Jennings painted several murals in Atlanta during the 1930s under the auspices of the WPA. He also designed stage sets, participated in Harmon Foundation exhibitions, taught at Atlanta University, and received a fellowship from the General Board of Education to study at the Rhode Island School of Design. Jennings completed numerous block prints and wood engravings during his time in Atlanta. Frederick Flemister produced a number of significant paintings during the forties. He depicted scenes of African-American life in the South using an expressionistic style influenced by Woodruff.

The publication of two of the earliest books devoted exclusively to African-American art, Alain Locke's *The Negro in Art: A Pictoral Record of the Artist* (1940) and James A. Porter's *Modern Negro Art* (1943) distinguished the 1940s. By the early 1950s African-American art had taken a different direction.

Celebration and Vision:

The Hewitt Collection of African-American Art

Biographies and Catalog

Charles H. Alston

Woman Washing Clothes, ca. 1970

oil pastel on paper

During the First World War, Charles Henry Alston's family moved from Charlotte, North Carolina, to New York City where he met Alain Locke, author of the influential anthology *The New Negro*, who introduced him to African sculpture.[1] Alston was also interested in the work of European modernists, such as Amedeo Modigliani, who employed forms derived from African art. The Mexican muralists such as Diego Rivera and José Orozco also influenced Alston.[2] Rivera's depictions of historical and contemporary Mexican struggles influenced many African-American artists who not only emulated the style but also embraced the idea that murals could engage issues such as racism.[3] Alston visited Rivera while he painted his controversial Rockefeller Center mural *Man at the Crossroads*.[4]

Artist George Biddle had seen the murals of Rivera, Orozco, and David Alfaro Siqueiros in Mexico and despite the Rockefeller Center controversy persuaded President Franklin D. Roosevelt to fund mural painting as part of the New Deal.[5] Under the Works Progress Administration (WPA), Alston was among the first African-American artists to execute a major mural project, *Magic and Medicine* (1935-36) for Harlem Hospital.[6] Alston, in collaboration with Hale Woodruff and other artists, completed a number of mural projects, including *Exploration and Colonization* and *Settlement and Development* (1948-49) executed for the black-owned Golden State Mutual Life Insurance Company in Los Angeles.[7] Significantly, many of these murals celebrated black history.

In the 1950s Alston began to work in an abstract style, although he never abandoned the figure. *The Family* (1955) in the Whitney Museum of American Art typifies both his style and his interest in depicting the family. He drew on his early interest in cubism, African sculpture, and a tendency to elongate forms reminiscent of Modigliani.

Alston proceeded as an abstract expressionist painter by first applying areas of color, and then as a representational painter by using line to delineate the volumes and contours of the human figures, thereby creating a tension between two- and three-dimensional space and between the non-objective and representational image.[8]

Alston varied the degree of abstraction, thereby allowing the subject to determine the style.

> More often than not, the painting tells me what it is going to be. All of my paintings start very abstractly. I just throw some color on the canvas, push it around, and then sit back and relax and look at it, and various patterns become suggestive...it becomes a conscious thing.[9]

In addition to his engagement with abstraction, Alston also explored the twinned notions of visibility and invisibility. An experience at a cocktail party prompted his consideration of vision. A white woman praised her black cook Cora, who had been in her employ for nineteen years. Alston asked, "What's Cora's last name?" The woman did not know. This encounter prompted Alston to represent faceless black figures in order to illustrate double consciousness—the psychological tension generated by the coexistence of African-American identity and racist assumptions. W. E. B. Du Bois has described this double consciousness as "a peculiar sensation...this sense of always looking at one's self through the eyes of others, of measuring one's soul by the tape of a world that looks on in amused contempt and pity."[10] In *Woman Washing Clothes*, the posture of the figure obscures her face. Alston's figuration demonstrates the influence of the Mexican muralists in the strong black outlines, the reduction of the body to geometric shapes, and the attributes which enhance the narrative.

David C. Hart

Romare Bearden

Jamming at the Savoy, ca. 1988

lithograph

His broad smile illuminated space, and he smiled frequently out of a deep joy for life and his passion to make art. Romare Howard Bearden (1912-1988) was an artist with a soul so big we could all climb inside. His collages were based on universal themes: family involved in the daily rituals of bathing, cooking, joy, or grief; sultry nights in sensually warm southern houses; the haunting blast of the distant train whistle bound for freedom; glimpses into city life laid bare by the dissolving of walls; the older woman as a source of wisdom and power; jazz.

Although he is known as one of the greatest American artists of his generation, he did not begin to make the collages that earned him recognition until a chance discovery in 1964. Bearden had been meeting with fellow African-American artists to discuss common aesthetic problems as well as the restrictions society imposed on their careers. Hale Woodruff named them the Spiral Group after the spiral of Archimedes as a symbol of their growth and hope. During one of these meetings someone suggested that they undertake a group project using cut-up photographs. Bearden grew very excited and proceeded to raid his wife Nanette's magazines for the following week's meeting. By the next week, everyone else had lost interest, but Bearden began to paste together compositions on his own. He would fracture the space in these pieces by varying the scale of his cutouts. He constructed faces by combining parts of faces from the magazines. This method allowed him to exaggerate eyes or mouths and to incorporate partial images of African sculpture. Encouraged by the possibilities, he had some of these small collages enlarged photographically. His dealer, Arn Elkstrom, mounted these *Projections* as the artist's next individual exhibition and the course of his future work was set. Bearden continued to make collages, along with a smaller body of watercolors, until his death at age seventy-six. Major change and growth occurred during that twenty-four-year period. The addition of color added punch to his rhythm, and he began to paint freely on and around the photographic areas. In many later collages he abandoned the photographic inclusions altogether.

Homage to Mary Lou, 1984

lithograph

Harlem Street Scene, ca. 1973

lithograph

To watch Bearden work in his Long Island studio was like watching the great jazz musicians whom he knew and loved. A blend of intuition and surety characterized his touch. There was very little hesitation about the placement of a scrap of paper or the addition of painted color. The structure of a consistent aesthetic vision that comes from experience was always present, but the spirit of improvisation kept the work fresh.

Consider *Morning Ritual* (1986). A rhythm section of warm and cool colors might be taking us to the baked red clay of his birthplace, Mecklenburg County, North Carolina, but we could be in any hot climate. Heat builds in the lower part of the collage, while the last vestige of evening cool flees from the interior. Let your eye dance to the rhythm of the shapes: the bright portion of the woman's body, the window, the shutter, the old broken tree flirting with the edge, the parked broom, and the chair. The horizontal white doorstep breaks the fall before yielding to the dog, whose muzzle reverses our direction and starts us all over again. The strong pull of the dark building expanding to the left would overwhelm the composition without the daring counterpoint of the brilliant red shutter. I can imagine Bearden's delight as he glued that renegade shape into place—perfect yet unexpected like the call and response of the blues. The cloud enters with the body language of the artist's brush, and we are swept through its billow to the upper left. Bearden was a master of the interval. Like the phrasing of a great jazz singer, his silences make the music.

He was quick to give credit to former teachers, especially George Grosz at the Art Students League. Grosz's advice to diagram the compositions of the masters gave Bearden a firm foundation for his own expression. The most unlikely influence, however, was his childhood friend Eugene, whom Bearden listed as his first drawing teacher and the reason art became a lifelong pursuit. Bearden befriended Eugene while living in Pittsburgh, Pennsylvania, with his maternal grandmother, Carrie Banks. One day Eugene showed Bearden his drawings on brown paper. Bearden was captivated, not least by the subject matter, which presented men and women in every possible sexual position. Eugene had depicted a brothel without exterior walls so that the viewer could see into every room. Bearden copied each drawing until the day his grandmother asked to see what the boys were doing at the kitchen table. She was outraged and destroyed the drawings, but the creative seed had been planted. She insisted that Eugene leave the bordello where his mother worked and live with them. When Bearden accompanied Eugene to his attic to retrieve his belongings, he saw the holes in the floor through which Eugene viewed his models.

Harlem Street Scene (ca. 1973) uses the revealed interiors often found in Bearden's urban collages. We see a pattern of activity both on the street and inside the houses, with many changes in scale to fracture the space. His emphasis on both public and private space draws attention to the myriad of activities that transpire when people live close together. Eugene would have been pleased.

In the 1930s, Bearden, Charles Alston, and others would go to the Savoy Ballroom where one could find the latest in jazz and dance. *Jamming at the Savoy* (ca. 1988) was one of many images that Bearden created to celebrate those free days full of sound. The rhythm is carried by light shapes coursing through a dark field. Strong diagonals either echo or form a counterpoint to the central guitar. Behind the dark rectangle is a cloudburst of color suggesting the mellow haze that results from an evening of ecstatic music.

I was in his apartment the night *Homage to Mary Lou* (1984) was delivered from the master printer. Bearden excitedly unwrapped the edition, which was to be sold as a benefit for his wife's dance company. When he revealed the lithograph, I could understand his passion. It is his finest print, exuding the warmth and touch of his collages. One can hear the music of the piano in the rhythm of the highly saturated colors and shapes. His admiration for previous masters, especially Henri Matisse, is clear. Nanette was concerned that the prints would not sell quickly at the established price.

Morning Ritual, 1986

collage with acrylic on plywood

I convinced her otherwise that night by purchasing the first one for the Davidson College art collection.

While sharing a rueben sandwich (one of his favorites) in Wolf's Delicatessen, I asked Bearden why he had kept the prices for his work so modest. He responded that he had all the money he needed to live—why ask for more? He also wanted his work to sell at auction for a price that was at or above the gallery's price in order to please his collectors. This modesty pervaded his life, and imbued him with immense generosity. Night or day he was available to young artists who sought his counsel. He never moved from his fifth-floor walk-up, and he maintained a small studio, formerly a dentist's office, in Long Island, which he reached by train each day. On the way to his studio one morning, he told me that he had learned two useful lessons from Matisse: never work more than three or four hours a day and never finish a piece at the end of the workday so the momentum would be there the next day.

Looking at a Bearden collage is like hearing the perfect note. His life experience gave him the eyes and the heart to imbue our daily existence with mythic significance. I loved Romare Bearden, and I wish he was still among us, but we have his body of work—a gift for all time.

Herb Jackson

John T. Biggers

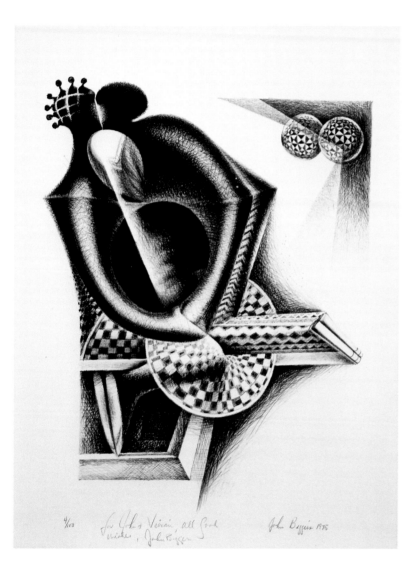

Family #2, 1975

lithograph

Family #1, 1974

charcoal on paper

John Biggers, internationally recognized as a leading educator and artist, is best known as an outstanding muralist. His accomplishments also include drawings, prints, easel paintings, sculptures, and book illustrations that celebrate linkage among the styles and cultures of Africa, the United States, and the rural South. Complex symbols and heritages coexist in the artist's work, ultimately expressing his humanistic vision of universal experience.

On 13 April 1924 Biggers was born into a large and closely knit family in the mill town of Gastonia, North Carolina.[1] He had planned to study plumbing at Virginia's Hampton Institute (now Hampton University) but in 1941 turned to art under the influence of his teacher, Viktor Lowenfeld, who encouraged studies of African and African-American art (a rarity at the time). Lowenfeld also introduced Biggers both to the American regionalists, who documented humble social scenes, and to the Mexican muralists, who invigorated this medium throughout the Americas. Biggers became acquainted with artists such as Charles White and Elizabeth Catlett as well as the Harlem Renaissance writers W. E. B. Du Bois and Alain Locke.[2] At Hampton, this "place of initiation," Biggers completed his first mural, *Dying Soldier* (1942), and his first painting, *Crossing the Bridge* (1942).[3]

Murals accommodate expansive narratives and their public presentation encourages civic enjoyment and edification. Biggers knew from personal experience that murals could reach a broader audience because as a young boy he had marveled at the huge Works Progress Administration (WPA) mural in Gastonia's post office.[4] In 1983 he completed *Family Unity*, a fifty-foot mural at Texas Southern University depicting continuity and progression from birth to death. His exploration of the family as a sacred unit prompted a turn toward geometric abstraction. Not surprisingly, Biggers' lithographs and drawings often derive from mural projects. Two images in the Hewitt Collection, *Family #1* (1974) and *Family #2* (1975), relate to figural groups in that mural.

After following Lowenfeld to Pennsylvania State University, Biggers earned bachelor's, master's, and doctoral degrees in art education by 1954.[5] He taught at Texas State University for Negroes (later Texas Southern University) in Houston from 1949 until his retirement in 1983. Biggers' emphasis on the exploration of cultural heritage marks both his teaching and his art. "The role of art," he believes, "is to express the triumphs of the human spirit" and "to express the profound beauty of the Afro-American people."[6]

Biggers' pilgrimage to West Africa in 1957 strongly affected his art. Funded by a UNESCO travel fellowship to study African traditions and cultures in Ghana, Dahomey, Nigeria, and Togo, the trip inspired an enormous body of work using African symbols and styles with less narrative content. In 1962 he published an award-winning visual diary of his African experiences titled *Ananse: Web of Life in Africa*. He recounts the "devastating" drama and beauty of Africa and discloses his fear that he would be unable to respond creatively to "this overwhelming country." *Ananse* remains an essential source for students of African-American art history because it was among the first texts to connect a contemporary black artist's life with the continent of his ancestors. This trip also prompted Biggers to explore abstraction, including the "sacred geometry" of African art such as Kuba textiles.[7]

The accent on circles in his lithograph, *Family #2*, demonstrates Biggers' commitment to formal elements that operate on both visual and metaphorical levels. Circles enliven the intimate scene and literally link man and woman, uniting the human and the celestial. The print may also allude to Akan symbols. Biggers wrote that during ceremonies the Akan sang: "The queen mother is the moon; the king is the sun." The circle unites binaries, such as man and woman, which echo the Chinese yin and yang. Biggers' trip to Africa, which he described as "the most significant of my life's experiences," enriched his art with new symbolic, formal, and personal dimensions. African textile designs, for instance, were similar to the lively patchwork quilts sewn by the women in his family. Given such cultural ties, viewers can enjoy what Biggers described as "a wonderful feeling of belonging."[8]

Twins of Morning, 1975

lithograph

Biggers' childhood in North Carolina is a constant source of inspiration. He affectionately remembers the "richness in culture—the music, the way people prayed and celebrated. That spirituality has been with me all my life."[9] Humble but potent icons of his childhood invade Biggers' work: the shotgun house where he was born (suggesting African-American vernacular architecture), the iron tubs his mother used to wash clothes (symbolizing purification), the anvil, the well, and the fireplace. These symbols, he writes, "are the magnificent objects that are known by individuals who have lived close to the earth...that I hope will convey universal meaning."[10] All three artworks in the Hewitt Collection emphasize family, lineage, and continuity. *Family #1* delicately delineates three clinging figures whose line and tonality link them as inseparable. Similarly, *Family #2* joins woman and man, mother and father. *Twins of Morning* (1975) depicts two youths and a man surrounded by the iconography that typifies Biggers' work.[11]

His art ennobles ordinary figures with dignity and grace. While much of his earlier work carried the sting of specific social commentary, he has transformed "his own anger into a more positive, universal outlook."[12] His ability to depict the strength of spirit in black culture while attempting to create universal symbols of regeneration is all the more remarkable given the racism he encountered as an art teacher in the South.[13] As Maya Angelou noted, Biggers' art allows "the discovery of ourselves at our most intimate level...[he]...sees our differences and celebrates them, and in doing so he allows the clans of the world to come together with deliberate and respectful appreciation."[14] Biggers integrates the past with the present, the mundane with the transcendent, African culture with African-American life in the South, European modernism with nonwestern art. His humanistic themes of community, family, and home emblematize an extended family that reaches beyond the confines of any region or continent. He mines a complex heritage born of cultural and personal memory to create symbols of life and spiritual vitality.

Lili Corbus Bezner

Margaret Burroughs

Warsaw, 1965

linocut

Best known as the guiding force behind the DuSable Museum of African-American History in Chicago, Illinois, Margaret Taylor Goss Burroughs has received international recognition as an artist, an educator, a poet, and a social activist. Born on 1 November 1917 in St. Rose Parish, Louisiana, she migrated to Chicago around 1920 with her parents, Alexander and Olivia Taylor, who like many African-Americans sought improved economic, educational, and social opportunities in northern cities after the First World War.[1] Burroughs graduated from Englewood High School in 1933 and began exhibiting at local art fairs while earning a teaching certificate in 1937 and an upper-grade art certificate in 1939, both from Chicago Normal College (now Chicago State University). After completing a B.F.A. in art education at the Art Institute of Chicago in 1946, as well as an M.F.A. in 1948, she began teaching art at DuSable High School, where she remained until 1969. Thereafter, she taught African-American art history and culture at local colleges and universities, including the Art Institute, Kennedy-King Community College, Elmhurst College, and Barat College. She also continued her formal education, studying at the School of Graphic Arts in Mexico City from 1952 to 1953 and pursuing doctoral studies at the Teachers College of Columbia University during the summers from 1958 to 1960.

Burroughs extended her education by traveling the globe, including numerous trips to Africa where she broadened her knowledge of indigenous cultures and collected items for the DuSable Museum. *Warsaw* (1965), a linocut in the Hewitt Collection, reflects her travels. During the year the artist spent at the School of Graphic Arts in Mexico, she studied printmaking under Leopoldo Mendez, an artist in the circle of Diego Rivera. True to the aims of the Mexican muralists, Burroughs produced works on paper in order to make art more accessible to those with limited means. In the summer of 1963, Margaret and Charles Burroughs, her husband, traveled to Montreal to board a Polish ship, which would take them to Holland, Poland, and the USSR. During the voyage, she spoke to a Polish government official, who offered to exhibit her work in the castle of Kosciusko, a famous Polish patriot who not only had fought in the American Revolution, but also donated to black education the American property he had received for his services.[2] *Warsaw* numbers among the images she made of the Polish and Moscovite church architecture which she saw on her journey through Eastern Europe.

In addition to teaching, painting, and printmaking, Burroughs also wrote and illustrated her first children's book, titled *Jasper, the Drummin' Boy*, in 1947. Other books followed, including *For Malcolm: Poems on the Life and the Death of Malcolm X* (1967) and *Africa, My Africa* (1970). For Burroughs, poetry not only preserved and celebrated black culture, but also served as an agent of change. In her poem, "What Shall I Tell My Children Who Are Black?" she vowed:

> I will lift up their heads in proud blackness
> With the story of their fathers and their fathers'
> Fathers. And I shall take them into a way back time
> Of Kings and Queens who ruled the Nile
> And measured the stars and discovered the
> Laws of mathematics. Upon whose backs have been built
> The wealth of two Continents. I will tell him
> This and more. And his heritage shall be his weapon.[3]

In addition to publishing her first book during the 1940s, Burroughs began exhibiting at more significant venues, such as the Atlanta Negro Exhibition (1947), where her print won an honorable mention, and the San Francisco Civic Museum (1949). She also contributed greatly to Chicago's black cultural renaissance, a counterpart of the Harlem Renaissance. She exhibited at the 1940 American Negro Exposition in Chicago and was instrumental in creating the South Side Community Art Center, a Works Progress Administration (WPA) project dedicated by Eleanor Roosevelt and Alain Locke.

Charles Burroughs, a poet and writer, was her partner in many endeavors, including the DuSable Museum.[4] The museum grew out of the couple's conviction that the educational establishment's omission of black history and culture must be rectified: "A museum shows kids they can be some-body," Burroughs said.[5] Founded by a small group of friends and estab-lished in three rooms of the Burroughs' south side home, the museum formally opened on 21 October 1961 as the Ebony Museum of Negro History and Art. "A lot of black museums have opened up," stated Burroughs, "but we're the only one that grew out of the indigenous black community. We weren't started by anybody downtown; we were started by ordinary folks."[6] More than 500 visitors toured the museum during the first year, prompting Burroughs to devote herself to fundraising.

In 1968 the museum was renamed in honor of Jean Baptiste Pointe DuSable, a man of African ancestry who was the first permanent settler in Chicago in the 1770s. In 1973 the museum moved to its permanent location, a former administration building donated by the city. The DuSable Museum disseminated information about black culture and history, emphasizing African heritage. In addition to programming cultur-al and educational events, the museum eventually housed a collection of more than 50,000 items including art, papers, books, artifacts, and memo-rabilia (such as the robe W. E. B. Du Bois wore to accept an honorary degree in Ghana).

Margaret Burroughs served as the museum's director until 1979, when she retired, assuming the position of director emerita. The DuSable Museum has served as a peg upon which Burroughs could hang her many efforts to promote black culture. She numbered among the founders of the National Conference of Artists at Atlanta University and served on the National Commission on Negro History and Culture. In 1980 she was one of ten African-American artists—including Romare Bearden, Ernest Crichlow, and Jacob Lawrence—honored at the White House by President Jimmy Carter.[7] She has also received a number of honorary doctorates in addition to other citations, honors, and commendations. More recent exhibitions of her work include *Two Centuries of Black American Art* (1976), a group exhibi-tion at the Corcoran Gallery of Art (1980), and a 1982 retrospective at the

Evans-Tibbs Collection in Washington, D.C.[8] Perhaps most importantly, she continues to advocate the role of women and minorities in the arts with her service on various commissions, boards, and committees, as well as with her art:

> I wish my art to speak not only for my people—but for all humanity...I am a humanist and glad to be. The whole motivation of my work...is, in the final essence, for the liberation of my people in particular and for the end of imperialist oppression of all the underprivileged peo-ple of the earth of all races, creeds and colors.[9]

Kristin U. Fedders

Elizabeth Catlett

Head of a Woman. 1967

lithograph

The lithograph *Head of a Woman* (1967) emblematizes Catlett's oeuvre. In this piece, Catlett isolated her subject's face in order to focus the woman's intense gaze on the viewer. Both the subject matter and the composition prioritize the black woman—who has historically been relegated to a secondary role in the art of Europe and the Americas—and accord her strength of character and intellectual self-sufficiency.

Catlett's interest in the black woman arises from her biography. Born Alice Elizabeth Catlett on 15 April 1915 in Washington, D.C., she was the third child born to schoolteachers John and Mary Catlett. Tragically, Catlett's father, who had instructed Booker T. Washington in mathematics at Tuskegee Institute before teaching in the public schools, died before her birth. Mary Catlett found menial work to support her three children, thus from an early age Elizabeth was familiar with the daily struggles of working-class black women. Having evinced an interest in the visual arts from childhood, Catlett attended art school after completing high school in 1931. She initially applied to the Carnegie Institute in Pittsburgh, Pennsylvania, but her application was denied. During the portfolio review, Catlett overheard faculty members saying that while she showed great talent, it was "too bad" that she was black. Following her mother's advice, Catlett applied to Howard University's art department. There she encountered a talented faculty who served as her earliest mentors. Under the influence of Lois Mailou Jones, James Porter, and department founder James Herring, she transferred her major from design to painting.

After her graduation in 1935, Catlett worked for two years as both an art program supervisor and an art teacher in the Durham, North Carolina, public schools while simultaneously fighting for better pay for black teachers. Tiring of these struggles and wanting to pursue her painting more seriously, she began an M.F.A. at the State University of Iowa (now the University of Iowa). The program offered two important advantages: no increase in tuition for out-of-state students and the opportunity to work closely with Grant Wood, the prominent American regionalist painter. She

also began to focus more intensely on sculpture, particularly the notoriously difficult medium of stone. In 1940 she became the university's first recipient of an M.F.A. in sculpture.

With her academic credentials in hand, she embarked on her earliest jobs teaching art at the university level. She first found work at the historically black Prairie View College in Texas and then briefly headed the art department at Dillard University in New Orleans, Louisiana, where she pioneered the use of live models. Leaving Dillard due to administrative conflicts, she and her new husband, printmaker Charles White, whom she had met while taking summer classes at the Art Institute of Chicago in 1941, moved to Manhattan. There the young couple's friends included cultural luminaries such as Ernest Crichlow, Jacob Lawrence, Charles Alston, Romare Bearden, Aaron Douglas, Langston Hughes, Ralph Ellison, and Paul Robeson. In New York, she continued her studies, pursuing lithography at the Art Students League and sculpture with Ossip Zadkine, whose cubist-based approach to sculpture influenced her work. Although he demonstrated the powerful interplay of negative and positive space, she argued that abstraction could not communicate with the wide group of viewers she wanted to address.

As rich as these various influences were, she could not devote herself full time to her art because she had to earn money. Her populist leanings always informed where and how she would earn money. Catlett spent several years teaching at Harlem's George Washington Carver School, an institution that offered inexpensive educational opportunities to working people. Her work at the school was part of a lifelong effort to address what she has termed "the cultural hunger" of American minorities, who had been offered either limited entrance or refused entrance to museums, symphony halls, and galleries.[1]

Increasingly frustrated with her inability to find time for her own work, in 1945 she secured a grant from the Julius Rosenwald Foundation in order to produce a series of prints, paintings, and sculptures of black women. She moved to Mexico City where she took a room in the home of Mexican muralist David Alfaro Siqueiros' mother-in-law. Through this connection, she met Siqueiros, Diego Rivera, and Frida Kahlo. Although she had moved to Mexico with her husband, the two soon returned to the United States to file for divorce. Catlett returned to Mexico alone. During the earlier trip, she and her husband had associated themselves with the Popular Graphic Workshop, a cooperative founded in 1937 in order to produce high-quality graphic art within the means all Mexican citizens. In addition to producing artistic prints, the workshop's members finished work for Mexican trade unions, student organizations, and anti-illiteracy campaigns.

In 1947 Catlett married Francisco "Pancho" Mora, a printmaker and colleague at the workshop. During the early years of their marriage, she gave birth to three sons. During their childhood, she limited her work to print-making until her youngest son entered kindergarten and she returned to sculpting. Catlett, who had never lost interest in three-dimensional work, studied with both Francisco Zuñiga and José Ruíz. Her lifelong work in this field was recognized in 1959 when she became the first woman professor of sculpture at the National School of Plastic Arts at the Free University of Mexico. Soon she was appointed director of the sculpture division.

Despite her professional success, Catlett's life in this period was not without difficulty. Her commitment to leftist causes in Mexico brought her to the attention of the House Un-American Activities Committee and she was harassed by U.S. officials in Mexico City. In 1962 she chose to become a Mexican citizen and was subsequently denied entry to the United States. Indeed, she was not granted a visa until 1971 when her individual exhibition, titled *Elizabeth Catlett*, opened at the Studio Museum in Harlem. During this difficult period, made more painful by the death of her mother in 1969, she created her most important work, *Homage to My Young Black Sisters* (1968).

In 1976 Catlett retired from full-time teaching and moved to Cuernavaca, Mexico. During her retirement she has continued to work, completing several large commissions. In 1978 she created a twenty-four-foot bronze relief titled *Students Aspire* for the Chemical Engineering Building at Howard University. Three years later, she completed life-sized portrait bronzes of José Vasconcelos and Jaime Torres Bodet for the Secretariat of Education in Mexico City. The same artist who was once rejected from the Carnegie Institute due to her race is today honored with exhibitions in Europe and the Americas and has received numerous honorary degrees.

Karen Kettering

Ernest Crichlow

Woman in a Blue Coat, ca. 1948

oil on canvas

Woman in a Yellow Dress, ca. 1980
collage with tempera on paper

Ernest Crichlow's inclination toward creative expression came from his
father, a plasterer and brick mason who copied comic strips, making the
characters come alive. Primarily a figurative painter, Crichlow has concen-
trated on those who live in his Brooklyn neighborhood: "I try to show all of
the emotions rather than just the conflict. I'm interested in clarity."[1] One
emotion, however, that stands out is entrapment. Barred by barbed wire,
banisters, or railings, or impeded by narrow windows, Crichlow's figures
express the limitations that many cannot overcome. "Our world is about
limitations. Sometimes we emerge, but then we seem to return again,"
Crichlow has said.[2] As a result, black faces, especially those of black children, are his focus.

Crichlow was born in Brooklyn, New York, on 19 June 1914 to Herbert and
Irene Crichlow, immigrants from Barbados.[3] At Haaren High School in
Brooklyn (now part of John Jay College), his art teacher, Florence
Newcomb, mentored him and gave him a job in the art department office,
where he dusted and read the books. Here he discovered black intellectuals
and artists such as Alain Locke, Countee Cullen, Aaron Douglas, and
Augusta Savage. After high school, he received a scholarship to attend
the Commercial Illustration School of Art. He made his first connection
with black artists when he went in search of Savage in her basement studio,
where he found her posing for Robert Savon Pious. Norman Lewis was
also present.[4] This encounter convinced Crichlow that he could become
an artist.

Joining the Harlem Artists Guild in the 1930s, Crichlow worked alongside
Jacob Lawrence, James Yeargans, Charles Alston, Henry W. Bannarn, and
Aaron Douglas.[5] He remained there for many years and also briefly taught
at the Savage Studio of Arts and Crafts. Unlike many of his artist-friends,
Crichlow had a family to support and continued his commercial work. His
relationship with the Harlem Art Center, a Works Progress Administration
(WPA) project, began around the same time that he illustrated book
jackets.[6] At the Center, Crichlow worked with most of the black artists in

New York at the time. He has said that the WPA brought artists together and provided recognition for their work, describing it as

> the greatest stimulant the American art scene has ever had. It meant something to be an artist then. The WPA was our haven and offered us a real entrée into what was happening. We had a lot of hope...Before that, very few of us had anything resembling a real art education.[7]

Like many WPA artists, Crichlow tackled political and social issues. Some of his most powerful and sensitive works harbor political content. In *Waiting* (ca. 1965), barbed wire restrains a young girl suggesting that external forces limit her opportunities. Her gaze reaches far beyond the restraining wire. Although imprisoned by her physical environment, she overcomes her situation with her mind. These pensive studies became signature works for Crichlow. His most well-known painting, *Woman in a Blue Coat* (ca. 1948), juxtaposes deep colors and light passages. Purchased from the artist by the Hewitts in 1980, the work was included in the exhibition, *Hidden Heritage: Afro-American Art, 1800-1950*.

Another area of interest has been his Caribbean heritage. Although his parents were Barbadian, his primary interest has been Jamaica. First visiting during their declaration of independence from the British Commonwealth, Crichlow was fascinated by the character of island people and visited regularly until the mid-1990s.[8] His interpretive realist style characterizes this group of works. *The Sisters* (1979) relies on the high contrast of dark skin with white clothing. Gray tones in the pleats of the clothing, background shapes, and palms soften the otherwise stark scene. Rhythmic movement characterized by subtle body language signals silent communication among the women. High contrast is also evident in *The Balcony* (1980).

Ernest Crichlow has been a strong advocate for black artists. In 1969 he, Romare Bearden, and Norman Lewis jointly founded the Cinque Gallery, which is devoted to the advancement of black artists. He has coauthored

Suburban Woman, 1979

collage with acrylic on paper

Ernest Crichlow

Boy in a Green Field, ca. 1979
acrylic on composition board

Girl with Flowers, ca. 1979
acrylic on composition board

several catalogues including *Fifteen under Forty: Paintings by Young New York State Black Artists* (1970). In 1976 he completed a mural depicting African-American history for the Boys and Girls High School in Brooklyn. The narrative not only illustrates the violence associated with the civil rights movement, but also offers hope for the future. In 1980 President Jimmy Carter honored Crichlow and nine other African-American artists at a White House ceremony for the National Conference of Artists.

Lizzetta LeFalle-Collins

The Sisters, 1979
serigraph

Street Princess, 1982
serigraph

Ernest Crichlow

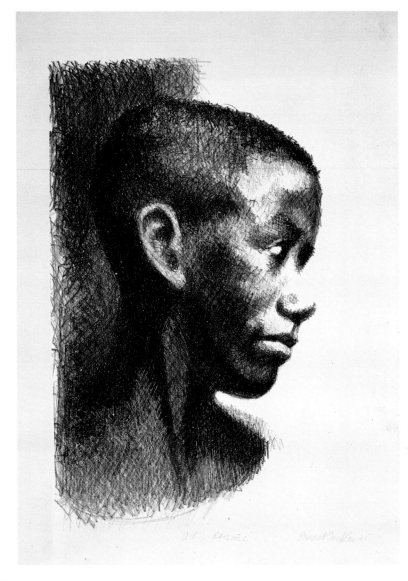

Ronnie, 1965

lithograph

Waiting, ca. 1965

lithograph

The Balcony, 1980

collage and acrylic on paper

James Denmark

Untitled . ca. 1983
watercolor

Like so many future painters and sculptors, James Denmark was born into a family of artists who nurtured his earliest interest in color, form, and design. Born in the small town of Winter Haven, Florida, on 23 March 1936, he grew up watching his paternal grandmother, Katie Denmark, as she crocheted, quilted, and constructed an innovative form of wire sculpture. She would bend a flexible, coated, and brightly colored wire acquired from the telephone company into patterns that resembled her crocheted work. Eventually her pieces—many of which are still in the artist's possession— grew to include complicated figures and narratives. Denmark's grandfather also served as a role model for his young grandson. Sylvester Denmark was a master bricklayer and was known for his specially designed molds made to decorate building facades.

Having grown up in such a fecund atmosphere, it is not surprising that James Denmark chose to study the visual arts at the historically black Florida Agricultural and Mechanical University in Tallahassee. Denmark entered the university's program in 1956 and supported himself with an athletic scholarship. While at the university, he worked closely with both prominent art historian Samella Lewis and Howard Lewis, head of the art department and a graduate of Ohio State University's program in industrial design. Denmark, a superior student, graduated with high honors.Because of his excellent performance, the department hired him as an adjunct instructor. He spent several years teaching courses for senior faculty on sabbatical and so was able to teach in every area the department offered— drawing, painting, sculpture, design, printmaking, and ceramics. After some discussion with his mentor, Howard Lewis, Denmark chose to apply to the M.F.A. program at the Pratt Institute in Brooklyn, New York. The program put him in close proximity to Manhattan's many galleries and museums and featured prominent faculty members such as Jacob Lawrence.

Denmark's path to the Pratt Institute was not as direct as he might have hoped. While an undergraduate, he met and married his first wife, Mary, and had a daughter, Wanda. Although the couple had divorced in 1961,

Daily Gossip, ca. 1975
collage on panel

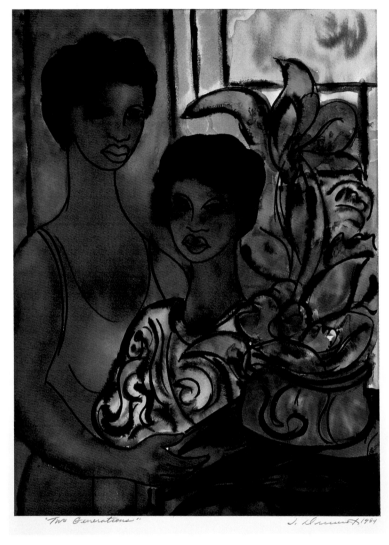

Two Generations, 1984

lithograph

Denmark not only had a child to support but also was faced with Pratt's tuition as well as New York rents. Because he had to save money for tuition, Denmark worked a variety of jobs while producing artwork in his spare time. Thus, by the time Denmark entered Pratt, he was already a mature and confident artist. Indeed, in December 1973, only three months after he had started graduate coursework, prominent art critic John Canaday favorably reviewed an exhibition of his work in the *New York Times*.[1] While at Pratt, Denmark worked most closely with Calvin Albert, a professor of sculpture. In addition, he soon came under the unofficial tutelage of Ernest Crichlow and Norman Lewis, both of whom lived nearby.

While living in New York both before starting school and while studying at Pratt, Denmark began to work extensively in collage. The Hewitt Collection contains two examples of this work: *Daily Gossip* (ca. 1975) and *Head* (1973). Contrary to many published sources, Denmark had been working with collage since he had been a student in Florida.[2] In New York, he began to work intensively with a variety of materials, including found objects and papers, in a manner that was reminiscent of his grandmother's quilts. In addition to the collages, the Hewitt Collection includes a lithograph, *Two Generations* (1984), and a watercolor, *Untitled* or *Woman with Red Hair* (ca. 1983). Besides demonstrating the artist's ease with a variety of media, the pieces typify his ability to render complex volumes and relationships with only a few expressive lines, as well as his sophisticated use of intense color.

Since his graduation from Pratt in 1976, Denmark has enjoyed a long and distinguished career. Almost immediately after he completed his degree, the Metropolitan Museum of Art acquired *Songbird*. In 1987 he was the first artist commissioned by the Seagram's Corporation to create a work based on his interpretation of the African-American family. Sales of Denmark's resulting work, *The Family*, supported the National Urban League's programs throughout the United States. More recently, the city of Charleston, South Carolina, commissioned him to create a poster for the MOJA Festival, an annual celebration of African-American culture. He is currently working on a series to benefit the Ronald McDonald House in Delaware. As Denmark is quick to point out, much of his success is based on the support of his second wife, Ethel, whom he married in 1984, and who has managed his studio and represented his work.

Karen Kettering

Head, 1973

collage

Jonathan Green

Easter, 1989
acrylic on paper

Painter and printmaker Jonathan Green was born in 1955 in Gardens Corner, South Carolina, the second of Ruth and Melvin Green's seven children. From the moment of his birth, Green was a special child. He was born with a caul—an inner fetal membrane covering the head at birth—that some believe is a sign "that the child is touched by an uncommonness and magic that will bring inordinate grace to the community."[1] His unique vision manifested itself early. As the artist told journalist Rick Compton, some of his earliest interest in design and form could be traced to his childhood chore of raking the front yard:

> I started becoming interested in the designs I could make with the rake. After awhile, the neighbors began commenting and asking if I could do some drawings for them. When my grandmother noticed I had talent, she bought me some paints.[2]

While his family remained supportive of his interests, he discovered that the larger community might not feel the same. When he won first place in a countywide art fair for a picture of Siamese kittens, the local newspaper would not print a story about him once the reporter discovered the grade-schooler was black.[3] At age 15, he along with his family moved to New York, where he suddenly had museums and libraries at his disposal. Green lived in the city for three years before returning with two of his siblings to Gardens Corner, where he was raised by his maternal grandparents, Eloise and Oscar Johnson.

Before applying to universities, he served in the United States Air Force, a job that took him to Texas, Colorado, and North Dakota. While initially he was assigned to duties as a chef, he was able to work with an Air Force illustrator and earned his certification as an illustrator. After completing his service in 1975, he spent several years both traveling and pursuing fabric design at the East Grand Forks Technical Institute in Grand Forks, Minnesota. Such a choice was imminently suitable. As his Air Force certification proved, he had mastered figural representation. Now he intensively studied the more abstract principles of color, form, and design. He divided his time between study and traveling, often throughout Mexico where he could examine both pre-Columbian art and Elizabeth Catlett's unique mixture of Mexican and African-American traditions. While his training in fabric design was useful—and Green later designed fabric for the Parisian House of Balmain—he entered a painting program at the Art Institute of Chicago in the fall of 1978.

Green was always a self-motivated, disciplined student. Immediately upon entering the Art Institute, he took a job as a security guard in the museum, which afforded him time to study the collection. He also volunteered at both the Goodman Theater and the Lyric Opera because it seemed essential as a student to be immersed in all aspects of the arts and to possess a well-rounded education. Despite these opportunities, the Art Institute still seemed somewhat barren because the traditions taught at the school and exhibited within the museum were decidedly Eurocentric. Beyond the classes of art historian Marilyn Houlberg and painter Emilio Cruz, he received most of his education in African and African-American visual traditions from alternate sources such as the South Side Community Arts Center.[4]

In a probing essay on that period of the artist's life, writer Ronne Hartfield has noted that in the "harsh gray realities of the urban north," Green sought to root himself in images from his past that spoke of both the Gullah culture of South Carolina and the African culture with which it is so closely connected.[5] Throughout his career, Green has made Gullah culture the subject of his figurative oil paintings. Geographical isolation and the fact that many of the Africans were brought from a small region of the West African Gold Coast meant that many cultural and linguistic traditions were preserved almost intact in South Carolina's Beaufort County. As Lynn Robertson, director of the McKissick Museum, observed, many of Green's paintings are based on personal recollections of traditions that have been preserved in his community.[6] These traditions are generally expressed through communal activities of work, worship, and social gatherings. The prime place held by communal religious activities is evident in *Easter* (1989), part of the Hewitt Collection.

Jonathan Green

Folding Sheets, 1989
acrylic on canvas

After graduating from the Art Institute in 1982, Green divided his time between further graduate study and traveling to Germany, Switzerland, and England. As he noted, the residents of these countries traditionally have been far more open to African and African-American cultural traditions than have Americans.

In the mid-1980s, he established a home in Florida. While he has continued to produce a prodigious body of paintings, he also devotes much of his energy to community service. Each year he produces a desk calendar illustrated with his paintings. Proceeds of the sale of the calendars are donated to charity. He also has participated in a program through which the Seagram's Corporation commissions artists to produce a work interpreting the black family, and all associated sales are donated to the National Urban League. The artist's contribution to this distinguished program was his 1989 lithograph *The Family*. Green has also served on the board of the American Express-sponsored Share Our Strengths, a charitable organization dedicated to assisting the homeless and to worldwide hunger relief. He also has worked with the Haitian Education and Revitalization Team, which builds primary schools in Haiti and then provides continuing support.

Most recently, Green has contributed to a number of projects that will make his work accessible and will aid in introducing young children to the visual arts. Since 1989 he has been furnishing illustrations for children's books. His first project, the book *Fathers and Sons*, was followed by *Noah* in 1995. In 1996 Green was one of seven artists selected to illustrate the seven principles of Kwanzaa for the children's book *It's Kwanzaa Time!* In the same year, Green provided the oil paintings used as illustrations for Dennis Hasely's *Crosby*. Hasely's text tells the story of a lonely, fatherless little boy who is able to reach beyond his isolation after he finds and repairs a broken kite. Critics widely praised the book for the sensitivity with which Green was able to render the often somber subjects addressed in the text.

Karen Kettering

J. Eugene Grigsby

Abstraction in Red and Black, ca. 1963

oil on canvas

J. Eugene Grigsby

The Enchantress, ca. 1979
lithograph

J. Eugene Grigsby's art incorporates numerous media, styles, and subjects. Primarily a painter and printmaker, he uses sources from African, Caribbean, Native American, and European art. As an internationally recognized and award-winning art educator for almost fifty years, Grigsby influenced hundreds, if not thousands, of students. His roles as both artist and educator are inseparable.

Grigsby was born in Greensboro, North Carolina, on 17 October 1918. His parents, both teachers, traveled throughout his childhood and settled in Charlotte, North Carolina, where he finished high school. After one year at Johnson C. Smith University in Charlotte, Grigsby transferred to Morehouse College in Atlanta, Georgia, where he studied art with his mentor, the influential educator and painter Hale Woodruff.[1] After graduating in 1938, he received a master's degree in 1940 from Ohio State University, where he had written a thesis on the influence of African art on modern art. Following Woodruff to his new post at New York University, Grigsby also earned a doctorate in art education in 1963 with a dissertation titled "African and Indian Masks." He also studied at the American Artists School in New York (1938-39), where he met an influential group of artists, including Jacob Lawrence and Romare Bearden, and the École des Beaux-Arts in Marseilles (1945).

After serving in the army, Grigsby taught both high school and college from 1946 to 1966. Throughout these years, Grigsby influenced many students and earned prestigious awards and honors. He was one of six artists selected by the Museum of Modern Art to represent the United States at the 1958 Brussels Universal and International Exposition. In 1988 he earned the designation National Art Educator of the Year from the National Art Education Association.

In addition to teaching media techniques and design aesthetics, Grigsby lectured widely on African and African-American art. He also exhibited works by Africans and African-Americans, often using his own personal collection. He organized *Encounters* in 1968 at Johnson C. Smith University, where he was a visiting curator. According to his catalogue, his purpose was to highlight outstanding works by infrequently exhibited American artists, especially black artists. Such work, he wrote, must be encouraged in every community in order to nourish talent and "discourage opposing spirits. There is growing demand by students in American schools for information about the black man who seems to have been invisible to most historians, and the artist has been among the most invisible."[2] For Grigsby, multicultural art enriches contemporary life because art contains "the soul of the community." Among his humanistic goals was the encouragement of "much needed cultural respect and self-image construction."[3] Grigsby's book, *Art and Ethnics: Background for Teaching Youth in a Pluralistic Society* (1977), numbers among the earliest texts on multicultural art. He celebrates such sources in his own work: for instance, Grigsby cites the stylistic influence of the Kwakiutl in *Specters* (1970).[4]

Grigsby favors acrylic painting and printmaking, including serigraphy, lithography, and woodcutting. Each work demonstrates his continuing concern for humanity, self, and heritage. Prompted by Hale Woodruff, Grigsby mined African, Hispanic, Native American, and European sources and styles. While many of his paintings and prints engage abstraction, he also works in a realist mode that "comes from a concern for conditions found among the least of us, especially the ones considered minority." Yet another group "concerns African mythology and imagery."[5]

Many of Grigsby's works visualize the struggles and triumphs of African-Americans. The legacy of social realism and civil rights imbues one woodcut in the Hewitt Collection. *No Vacancy* (ca. 1979) depicts a black family turned away from a whites-only hotel. The strong contrast of black and white dramatizes the woodcut both literally and metaphorically. White-hooded images of looming Ku Klux Klan members crowd behind the tightly centered family, and one skeletal face projects death and danger. Like the Holy Family, this family can find no place to rest. According to Grigsby,

African Journey: The Bridge, ca. 1981

serigraph

Specters, 1970

oil on canvas

J. Eugene Grigsby

Black, Brown and Beige, 1963
oil on canvas

such works express "my concern for the conditions under which people live, particularly the less fortunate." Blending this concern "for people and the search for heritage" with strong formal design, Grigsby creates some of his most forceful figurative work.[6]

While on sabbatical in 1972, Grigsby traveled throughout Africa and lectured on African and African-American art. African-inspired themes intensified in his work, as seen in his series paying homage to Bolongongo, the Kuba patron saint, or the series on the Orisha of Yoruba.[7] The *African*

Journey series is represented in the Hewitt Collection by *The Bridge* (ca. 1981), a serigraph visualizing the symbolic bridge between the Americas and Africa. Shown here as a material connection between continents, the bridge evokes both painful and positive histories of this connection including the Diaspora, slave ships, and the dissemination of artistic traditions to new generations in new lands.

Grigsby's work often depicts specifically West African icons. His images of Yemaya (or Yemanja) concern the Orisha, emissaries of God who rule over the forces of nature, according to Yoruba myths. Yemaya, the female figure in his lithograph *The Enchantress* (ca. 1979), rules over the seas and lakes as the mother of all humanity and is also associated with the moon, fertility, and labor. Brought to the New World by slave descendants in Cuba and Brazil, Yemaya, through her attributes, offers comfort and sustenance. Grigsby's Yemaya dominates the picture plane, as fluid as water and as vibrant as tropical plumage.

The largest portion of Grigsby's work is abstract. More than formal investigations, these works chronicle inner views and personal dimensions. He notes that *Black, Brown, and Beige* (1963) was influenced by the music of Duke Ellington. *Abstraction in Red and Black* (ca. 1963) is part of a series exploring color relationships, an aspect of Woodruff's instruction that profoundly influenced Grigsby's self-explorations through design.[8]

Grigsby's sources, whether modernist or African, enrich an eclectic body of work, which he described as a rich stew. Such works, he wrote, are "remarkably delicious when all ingredients are respected and admired for their differences and for what they add to the flavor. When parts are unknown, feared, or not respected, the taste is not so pleasing." Ever the educator, Grigsby believes that only with increased understanding and exploration of diverse sources can artists "seek greater humaneness through cultural identity, recognition, and self-respect."[9]

Lili Corbus Bezner

No Vacancy, ca. 1979

woodcut

Inner View, ca. 1978

lithograph

Earl Hill

Beulah's World , 1968

oil on composition board

As the civil rights movement gained momentum, greater numbers of black artists organized. Art became a vehicle for the expression of the ideals of equality, integration, and independence. Groups of artists worked to counteract the slow pace at which museums and galleries were recognizing black art and artists.[1] Some artists called for a representational art that would document the lives of ordinary people. Accordingly, Earl Hill, who participated in a local group of artists, chronicled modest human activities.

Hill was born in New York in 1927, but spent much of his youth in Bells Mills, a town in rural Virginia. After returning to New York, Hill graduated from New York University—where he took classes with Hale Woodruff—with a degree in education in 1951. In 1960 he received a master's degree from the City College of New York. He taught art appreciation in public schools in New York, Baltimore, and the Virgin Islands. Throughout his career, he refined his painting skills, taking classes at the Art Students League, the Pratt Institute, and the College of the Virgin Islands in St. Thomas. With Ruppert Murray, he co-owned the Studio Gallery in Mount Vernon, New York, during the 1960s. He exhibited at various venues, including the Black Art Museum in Hempstead, New York, the Riis Gallery in St. Thomas, and the Great Neck Public Library in Great Neck, New York. He retired from teaching in 1984, a year before his death.[2]

In both his teaching and his art, he attempted to foster an understanding of the humanity of the black community. In a 1986 review of an exhibition of the Long Island Black Artists Association, Helen A. Harrison, a critic for the *New York Times*, described Hill's painting, *The Bag Lady*. Harrison wrote that "she almost merges with the background, as she frequently does in reality, but her loneliness is relieved by the birds that share her bench, as if to inject a hopeful note in an otherwise sad vignette."[3]

Hill's other works from the sixties similarly emphasized the humanity of the ordinary individual. *Weight of the World* (1967) is a quiet and sensitive portrayal of a black woman contemplating the burdens that many women

The Presence. 1974

oil on wood

Weight of the World, 1967
watercolor

face. The watercolor depicts a black woman sitting on a folding chair that one might find in a church basement. She is dressed in simple but formal attire: a skirt, a handbag, a blouse buttoned to the neck, and a cardigan draped over her shoulders. She rests her chin on her hand and gazes blankly off into space while contemplating her troubles. Her closed posture reflects her mood. No context distracts the viewer from the figure that fills the frame, focusing attention on the subject.

Hill uses irony to rework canonical images, a strategy exemplified by *Beulah's World* or *The Gleaners* (1968). The title *Beulah's World* perhaps invokes Andrew Wyeth's *Christina's World*, the famous painting in which a young woman in a grassy field seemingly crawls toward a distant house. For the ambiguous figure of Christina, Hill substituted two black women, whose "world" consists of labor. Moreover, the name "Beulah" had been popularized as a black woman's name by the 1950s television show featuring a black maid. The work's second title, *The Gleaners*, refers to Jean-François Millet's celebrated image of French peasants. Hill's women assume the posture of Millet's gleaners, however the style derives from the modernist tradition, including that practiced by Romare Bearden.[4]

The Presence (1974) depicts the artist's daughter, Paula, at age nine. Hill captured his daughter's energy by using pose and execution to engender a sense of movement and dynamism. The narrow, vertical format focuses attention on her movement. The figure emerges from a fractured, unspecific background, which intensifies the illusion of movement. Her bent knees, flying braids, and dynamic pose further emphasize action.

David C. Hart

Alvin C. Hollingsworth

Family Tree, ca. 1977

lithograph

Born in Harlem around 1928 and raised in a tenement, Alvin C. Hollingsworth draws upon his urban experience for many of the images and themes that animate his work.[1] His West Indian parents instilled a strong work ethic that when combined with his prodigious energy has resulted in his engagement with media ranging from collage to television to poetry. Nevertheless, painting and printmaking most often convey his subjects including biblical themes, women, the city, and the role of the African-American artist.

Hollingsworth became interested in art at an early age. His first after-school job was helping Chick Quinlan to produce the comic strip *Cat Man*. By the time he graduated from the High School of Music and Art, he had a thriving business drawing his own cartoons and working on syndicated comics such as *Superman* and *Batman*.[2] He majored in art at the City College of New York (CCNY), graduating in 1956 as a Phi Beta Kappa. While pursuing abstract expressionism, he continued to earn money by doing illustrations for magazines such as *Playboy* and *Swank*. To further supplement his income, he not only executed paintings to order, sometimes making sixteen or more of the same image, but also began teaching at a junior high school in the Bronx. After earning his master's degree from CCNY in 1959, he mounted his first individual show at the Ward Eggleston Gallery, New York, in 1961. According to Hollingsworth, the subsequent *Cry City* exhibition heralded change: "At that point I vowed that I would never compromise my art again. The *Cry City* show in 1965 was strong, direct, ugly—and a financial disaster. But I did not compromise then, and I will not compromise now."[3]

Combining graphic and painterly qualities, the four works in the Hewitt Collection typify Hollingsworth's mature style. Both *Tomorrow* (ca. 1977) and *African Village* (ca. 1978) couple oil washes with India ink, joining the artist's early abstract expressionist tendencies with the graphic sensibility he had honed as an illustrator. Expressive inked lines and washes of rich color coalesce into elongated, simplified, regal bodies with finely

articulated hands and heads. The pyramidal compositions structuring *Tomorrow*, *Waiting #2* (ca. 1977), and *Family Tree* (ca. 1977) not only evoke the monumental figural compositions of the Italian Renaissance, but also suggest striving and growth.

Hollingsworth also engaged contemporary issues, including feminism, the city, and the role of the African-American artist. In 1971, he focused on *The Women*, a series of paintings and poems created as "songs of freedom and equality" developed from a sequence of interviews with fourteen women artists.[4] He said: "I take my hat off doubly to the black woman...I wanted people to recognize the pride of women, the spiritual qualities of women, the sacrifices of women."[5] The images in the Hewitt Collection reflect Hollingsworth's ongoing engagement with this theme. *African Village* depicts a busy community of women and children pursuing quotidian activities. Similarly, *Family Tree* celebrates the family as the basis upon which children thrive. *Tomorrow* and *Waiting #2* present a more iconic vision of woman and child. The women—tall, regal, and dressed in traditional robes—evoke the physiognomy of the Watusi, while both the subject and the pyramidal composition recall Renaissance images of the Holy Family.[6]

The social consciousness that characterizes Hollingsworth's images of women underpins his oeuvre. Around 1963 Hollingsworth and twelve other African-American artists, including Romare Bearden and Charles Alston, founded the Spiral Group. The group's goal was not only to support the civil rights movement, but also to discuss whether the African-American artist imparts a unique aesthetic quality to art, an essence dubbed variously the "signature," the "thumbprint," and the "Negro image." A group interview published in *Art News* in 1966 documents the various opinions held by group members, including Hollingsworth's interest in artistic issues transcending race. Hollingsworth pondered: "I wonder why it should be necessary to seek one particular image. Even the exponents of Pop Art paint in divergent ways." Describing Spiral as "a form of group therapy," he identified the group as "a place for Negroes to air their own prejudices and see

Waiting #2, ca. 1977

oil and acrylic collage

Tomorrow, ca. 1977

oil and India ink on canvas board

each other in realistic terms and realize that we have the same concerns as most bourgeois white painters."[7] Similarly, in his poem, "The Prophet's Ode," he exclaimed:

> The difference one sees in black
> and white proves there is
> no difference at all!!![8]

Hollingsworth's philosophy has prompted some writers to group him with the so-called Blackstream Artists, African-American artists who emphasized connections rather than differences between ethnic groups.[9]

Although Hollingsworth explores the experience of African-Americans, his work also engages broader art historical trends, including figurative expressionism and assemblage, both responses to abstract expressionism. During the 1950s in New York, a younger generation of painters—including Lester Johnson, Larry Rivers, and Bob Thompson—combined figural subjects, urban themes, and expressionistic style in an effort to relate abstract expressionism to contemporary experience.[10] Hollingsworth, who had pursued abstract expressionism during the 1950s and early 1960s, embraced the trend toward figurative expressionism, combining sweeps of color with modulated line in order to articulate the urban experience of African-Americans. *Tomorrow* maintains that expressive tradition. Washes of color outline the figures, pooling with greater intensity around the heads, while inky lines delineate hands and heads, including the forceful silhouette of a black woman, a favored motif that invests this figurative composition with specific meaning.

In addition to working in a figurative and expressionistic mode, Hollingsworth also has explored assemblage, another artistic trend of the late 1950s and early 1960s. As a doctoral candidate at New York University, Hollingsworth experimented with the use of fluorescent materials in conjunction with ultraviolet light, installing an "art room" equipped with a mirror and an ultraviolet light that made the viewer's reflection

African Village, ca. 1978

India ink and oil on canvas

appear black.[11] Like the assemblages of street junk first exhibited in the late 1950s by artists such as Allan Kaprow and Robert Rauschenberg, Hollingsworth's assemblages introduced to the gallery the detritus of urban life, including piano keys, fish bones, teeth, and hangers.[12] Similarly, *Waiting #2*, an oil and acrylic collage, uses multiple media to extend the artist's range of expression.

A versatile and energetic artist, Hollingsworth has written and illustrated a book for children, written articles, written and hosted television shows, lectured, and supervised educational projects, as well as teaching and exhibiting artworks. While advocating the position of the African-American artist through his own work and group efforts such as Spiral, he has asserted the value of broad artistic experience. In 1968 Hollingsworth wrote,

> Having to learn the current art styles and yet having the girth of Black experience to draw from puts the Black artist in a unique position. He had learned the background and technical skills of his art and developed a voice so resounding it had to be heard.[13]

The same combination of experience and currentness characterizes the four images included in the Hewitt Collection.

Kristin U. Fedders

Ronald Joseph

Two Musicians, 1952-55

lithograph

Because Ronald Joseph spent most of his career in Belgium, historians have often overlooked his work despite his pursuit of abstraction after the Second World War when critics, museums, and art historians anointed abstract expressionism as the dominant American style. Perhaps more surprisingly, many standard texts on African-American art also omit Joseph or mention him briefly. Although he exhibited at the Metropolitan Museum of Art at the age of eighteen, participated in the Harlem Renaissance, and worked in an abstract expressionist mode, Joseph has yet to receive the recognition attained by many of his fellow artists, including Charles Alston and Hale Woodruff.

Joseph was born in 1910 in St. Kitts in the British West Indies. His mother, a charwoman, gave the infant to Theophilus and Henrietta Joseph, with whom he moved to New York City around 1920. There he attended public school and distinguished himself as a talented draftsman. His drawing teacher referred him to Henry E. Fritz's experimental art class, held on Saturdays at Peter Stuyvesant High School. Fritz also arranged for Joseph to attend the Ethical Culture School, where he pursued the fine arts. In 1929, as part of Fritz's annual exhibition at the Metropolitan Museum of Art of the work of thirty of the most gifted public-school students, Joseph exhibited sixty watercolors, charcoals, and crayon drawings, many of sporting figures. He was the first student to be honored with such a focus. A newspaper article, titled "Negro Boy Artist Aims to Equal Whites; Ability to Portray Action Amazes Critics," quoted the artist: "I want to show any white man that I can do anything that he can. The negro is beginning to do that." The reporter also characterized the artist as one who "wants to paint forces and effects rather than people," a comment that presaged Joseph's interest in abstraction. In the early 1930s, Joseph attended the Pratt Institute for three years, while living with his foster parents in order to save money.[1]

During the 1930s and 1940s, Joseph participated in the Harlem Artists Guild, the Works Progress Administration (WPA) mural project, and vari-

The Family, ca. 1953

mixed media on paper

ous exhibitions of African-American art. During the Depression, both
the disruption of social patterns and the federally funded art projects
allowed African-American artists unprecedented access to training, public
exposure, and work. Black artists not only worked with nationally known
figures—including George Bellows, Thomas Hart Benton, and José Orozco—
but also had the opportunity to develop both skills and ideas. In addition,
the WPA placed few restrictions on its artists, enabling African-Americans
to depict subjects ranging from lynching to black neighborhoods. Ronald
Joseph worked on the WPA Harlem Hospital murals (under the direction of
Charles Alston) and as an instructor at the Harlem Community Center, the
largest WPA art project in the country. He became a representative of the
Harlem Artists Guild, a union founded in 1935 to represent black artists
who had been denied supervisory status in the WPA.[2] Joseph also exhibited
at the Harlem Art Center in 1938 and 1939, in the *Contemporary Negro Art*
exhibition mounted by the Baltimore Museum of Art in 1939, and at the
American Negro Exposition held in Chicago in 1940.[3]

After serving in the Air Force as a member of the ground crew at Tuskegee
during the Second World War, Joseph studied art in Peru and in Paris while
supported by the Rosenwald Fellowship and a GI Bill of Rights scholarship.
He also studied in Mexico. After the war, the critical acclaim lavished on
abstract expressionism as the epitome of modern, white male creativity did
not encompass Joseph, who worked menial jobs in order to survive.[4] In
1956 Joseph borrowed money from printmaker Bob Blackburn and moved
to Belgium, where he was successful. The three works in the Hewitt
Collection date from the period immediately before his departure and
demonstrate not only his commitment to abstraction, but also the strong
compositions, expressive forms, and balanced colors that prompted James
A. Porter to describe Joseph as "our foremost Negro abstractionist."[5]

Joseph described his artistic project as an effort to express himself "in
terms of elementals. I wanted to find out to what extent I could paint a
painting from the inside—the inside of me." His work evinces a broad

Still Life, 1950-54

mixed media on paper

familiarity with modes of abstraction ranging from cubism to Chinese painting. *Still Life* (1950-54) demonstrates his interest in the cubism of Pablo Picasso, Georges Braque, and Juan Gris, who "knocked me into a corner because of his logic and his interest in form."[6] However, unlike the monochromatic compositions of the cubists, Joseph uses color, as well as form, to structure *Still Life*. Blue elements in the foreground, middle ground, and background knit together the compositional planes. Similarly, the red table extends toward the orange panel that defines the background, forging a passage through the crowded space. White provides a striking contrast to the rich earth tones and vibrant colors and offers a point of entry into the dense composition.

Two Musicians (1952-55) suggests the fractured figures of Picasso (*Three Musicians* [1921] and *Seated Bather* [1930]). Joseph carved the figures from the paper like a sculptor carving a relief. The bodies seem intertwined and legs and hands appear in silhouette. Both the bulging white shapes pressed against the frame and the black, white, and ocher palette evoke Robert Motherwell's *Elegy to the Spanish Republic* series (initiated in 1949 with *At Five in the Afternoon*). The title imbues these figures with a specific identity as musicians, although the compositional logic of white figures on a black background with overlapping black figural elements confounds any attempt to identify racial characteristics and suggests that skill, rather than race, characterizes the musician—and the artist.

In contrast to *Two Musicians*, *The Family* (ca. 1953) clearly depicts African-American figures. Mother and child are joined in the foreground, while the father stands behind them, his partially colored face emerging tenuously from the background. Although it is tempting to identify this fragmented figure with the artist, whose race impeded his public recognition, the compelling figural presentation may have been driven by compositional concerns. The circular format recalls other familial representations, such as Renaissance tondi depicting the Holy Family, as well as Robert Delauney's experiments with orphic cubism.

After relocating to Belgium in 1956, Joseph seldom exhibited in the United States. Although writers frequently omitted him from surveys of the Harlem Renaissance, African-American art, and abstract expressionism, Ann Gibson, a scholar of abstract expressionism, contacted Joseph in Belgium in 1988. The artist said that "just when [my painting] became something rather direct and clear, I was called by Ann Gibson. I thought a miracle had happened..."[7] The following year, he traveled to the United States to participate in a panel discussion of "Black Printmakers and the WPA," which included his friend Bob Blackburn, who had arranged the sale of some drawings—including these three—to fund the artist's trip. Although he had planned future exhibits of his work in the United States, he died in 1992.

Kristin U. Fedders

Jacob Lawrence

Playing Records , 1949

India ink on paper

Painter Jacob Lawrence is a master storyteller as well as a master of compositional design whose complicated method of figurative abstraction challenges art afficionados without alienating laymen. Lawrence has made a career of communicating black experiences through his visual narratives based on African-American history and culture. His interest in history and his conviction that the story of African-Americans had not been adequately addressed in American history books encouraged his production of series. He decided to use a storyboard format because he felt that one image offered insufficient room to tell the stories. These culturally centered works have universal appeal because they deal with issues of resistance and triumph.

Lawrence was born in Atlantic City, New Jersey, on 7 September 1917 and as a toddler, moved to Easton, Pennsylvania, with his family. His father was a cook for the railroad and rarely at home. His mother was a domestic laborer. By the time Lawrence was seven years old, his father had abandoned them, and his mother moved the children to Philadelphia before finally moving to Harlem around 1930 in the midst of the Harlem Renaissance. His mother enrolled him in an after-school art workshop at the Utopia Children's Home Neighborhood House where Charles Alston and Henry W. Bannarn mentored him. He dropped out of high school after two years due to both the lack of encouragement and the need to help support his family.[1] Nevertheless, he was now considering a career in art. He later said, "I may have been working at a print shop and delivering laundry, but all I was *thinking* of was art."[2] After taking art classes at various community art workshops and spending six months with the Civilian Conservation Corps, Lawrence received a two-year scholarship through Harry Gotlieb, president of the Artists Union, to attend the American Artists School in 1937. He studied with Anton Refregier, Sol Wilson, and Eugene Moreley and received help from the Harlem Artists Guild. In 1938 he had his first individual exhibition sponsored by the James Weldon Johnson Literary Guild at the Harlem YMCA. He also produced his first series, *Toussaint L'Ouverture*, based on the life of the Haitian independence leader.

Near the end of 1938, Augusta Savage helped Lawrence obtain his first job with the Works Progress Administration (WPA) during which he painted the *Frederick Douglass* and *Harriet Tubman* series. Of his serial works, Lawrence later stated,

> I guess I was impressed by everything in my environment without even knowing it…and I was interested in story telling. As a young artist, I wasn't getting big mural commissions, naturally, so the way I thought to tell the story of a person's life was through a series of panels, a little like comics.[3]

These serial works share striking similarities: all are based on resistance to slavery as a means of survival; they celebrate the notion that one person can change the course of history; and their formal characteristics are based on an architectonic compositional structure composed of geometric forms and vivid colors. They narrate stories of black heroes constantly moving toward independence and opportunity. After the WPA, Lawrence continued the series format. He became the most celebrated African-American artist of the period, winning second prize in the 1940 American Negro Exposition in Chicago, Illinois, and mounting both an individual exhibition at the Baltimore Museum of Art in 1939 and an exhibition at Columbia University in 1940.

After the First World War, the reality of the mass migration of blacks from the South to the North prompted an even more personal series. *The Migration of the Negro Series* (1940-41) consists of sixty panels that portray the mass migration that literally affected all African-Americans, including those who migrated to the North, those already living there, and the many who remained in the South. Lawrence stated: "At that time very few blacks were born in the North. And if they were, their parents surely weren't. To me it was a dramatic event my parents and I were a part of, just as we were part of Harriet Tubman's escape."[4] The year 1941 also marked his marriage to his artist-friend Gwendolyn Knight, whom he had known since his early days at the Harlem Art Workshop. She has been a constant source of psychological strength and stability and guided his artistic career.

Continuing to explore the serial format, Lawrence completed *Harlem* (1942-43) and *War* (1946-47), a result of his service in the Coast Guard from 1943 to 1945. In 1947 *Fortune* commissioned him to travel to the South to create postwar images of blacks, a project that yielded a series of ten pictures titled *In the Heart of the Black Belt*. Concurrently, he created book illustrations in black-and-white gouache for Langston Hughes' book of poems, *One Way Ticket* (1949), which addressed the black migration. An illustration titled *Playing Records* or *The Disc Jockey* (1949), originally intended for the book, was given as a gift to the Hewitts from John Hewitt's sister in 1979. This drawing speaks to the new urban music that flourished in northern cites. In *Playing Records* smoke streams from a cigarette held by a goateed, beret-wearing disc jockey who guards a turntable. Two more music afficionados, one wearing dark glasses and the other a beret, stand behind the disc jockey. The threesome epitomizes the essence of urban cool, and one can surmise by their attributes and attitudes that their music of choice is jazz.

Both this art production and the acclaim took its toll on Lawrence and in 1949 he voluntarily underwent therapy at Hillside Hospital in Queens, New York. This period of rest and reflection yielded a series of ten paintings titled *Hospital Series* (1950). Once released in 1950, Lawrence continued his commitment to social commentary. In 1955 Lawrence began a series of sixty tempera paintings titled *Struggle: From the History of the American People* (1955-56), which illustrated American conflicts from the Revolutionary War to racial clashes. Nonserial works such as Lawrence's *Invisible Man Among the Scholars* (1963) highlighted the loneliness felt by the few blacks attending historically white universities. The *Ordeal of Alice* (1963) depicts a girl standing in an arrow-pierced white dress, clutching her books while ghoulish segregationists taunt her.

In 1972 Lawrence and his wife left Harlem for Seattle, Washington, where he became a professor of art at the University of Washington. In the 1940s he had begun to create compositions that depicted manual labor, specifi-
cally the work of carpenters, and this subject continued to attract him in his new home. He constructed his carpenters like multistoried structures. Lawrence also collects carpentry tools which he neatly displays on shelves in his studio. He has explained his love for tools with this anecdote:

> When I was about 15 or 16, I was exposed to the workshop of these three brothers in Harlem, cabinetmakers. I got to know them, and they got to know me. For me, tools became extensions of hands, and movements.[5]

Similarly, Harriet Tubman's large hands function as tools as she cuts wood in the seventh image in the series.[6] Her hands magnify her physical strength as her body dominates the picture plane. As a master storyteller, Lawrence creates works that are accessible, uncompromising, and driven by his empathy with those he portrays.

Lizzetta LeFalle-Collins

Hughie Lee-Smith

Signaler II, 1983
oil on canvas

Hughie Lee-Smith's paintings have had a surprising influence on the art world. The combination of traditional realist style with mysterious, ambiguous content has prompted many viewers to describe the images in vague and subjective terms. Moreover, the critical response reflects the problems affecting many African-American artists: Lee-Smith has never received the recognition accorded many white artists, and by painting universal rather than black subjects he has been often overlooked as a black artist.

Lee-Smith was born in 1915 in Eustis, Florida.[1] His parents supported his artistic interests by encouraging his participation in various organizations in the cities to which they moved.[2] Lee-Smith has said:

> My own experience is hardly typical, however. My parents just hap-
> pened to be very interested in this sort of thing—creativity, I mean—
> and I had quite a bit of encouragement. Theater training as a
> youngster, quite a bit of modern dance in the thirties. Then I won a
> scholarship to the Cleveland School of Art.[3]

Lee-Smith even founded an interracial modern dance group during the thirties, demonstrating the range of artistic interests that attracted him.[4] He graduated from the Cleveland Institute of Art in 1938.

During the Depression, Lee-Smith began his painting career through the Works Progress Administration (WPA)—which employed artists who might ordinarily have received no support—and developed two enduring interests: realist painting and teaching art. Commenting on *Artist's Life I* (1939), a work he completed during this period, Lee-Smith described the struggle to reconcile art and social involvement when he said: "the artist with a canvas [is] choosing between the non-involvement of studio painting…and…class struggle…"[5] During the Second World War, Lee-Smith continued to paint while working in a Ford factory before joining the Navy in 1944.[6] He attempted to combine art and life in such projects as the 1947 mural *The History of the Negro in the U.S. Navy* (1947) at the Great Lakes Naval Training Center near Chicago, Illinois.[7] After the war, he lived in both Detroit,

Michigan, and New York, painting, teaching, and winning a number of awards. He taught during the following decades at prestigious schools such as the Art Students League in New York, the Studio-on-the-Canal in Princeton, New Jersey, and at Howard University, Washington, D.C., as artist-in-residence, where he headed a student mural project on campus in 1970.

Lee-Smith mounted his first retrospective exhibition in 1988 at the New Jersey State Museum. Both the retrospective and a growing number of group and individual exhibitions have inserted the artist's name into the modernist canon. In 1994 he received the commission for a portrait of Mayor David Dinkins (now displayed at City Hall in Manhattan). His emphasis on representation probably contributed in part to the lack of recognition early in his career when critics favored abstraction. The artist's postwar work favored dreamlike imagery, as well as personal iconography. Some recurring elements include ribbons twirling in the breeze, walls cracking and crumbling, and solitary figures turned away from the viewer. Lee-Smith's combination of skilled representation and elusive content has prompted many viewers to describe his style as magic realism, classicism, or romantic realism.[8] Lee-Smith has described his work more simply: "As an artist, I'm always trying to change things from what they are."[9] Although his representational style initially seems accessible, his obscure subjects resist interpretation. *Signaler II* (1983) reflects the contemplative tenor and realist subject matter of his later works. Although the work is small in scale, it gives "the full feeling of the larger pieces" according to the Hewitts, who purchased the work for this reason.[10]

Kirstin Ringelberg

Virginia Evans Smit

Harlem Games, ca. 1964
woodcut

Virginia Evans Smit continually expands the expectations and definitions of printmaking through her innovative techniques and vision. She is also an eloquent spokesperson and teacher of art. Born in Philadelphia, Pennsylvania, in 1936, she began her artistic education by watching her father paint as well as taking weekend art courses at the Philadelphia Museum of Art. After receiving a degree in art education at Morgan State College, Smit enrolled in the M.F.A. program at the University of Pennsylvania where she won the prestigious Thorton Oakley Creative Achievement Award for her student work. This recognition, says Smit, encouraged her to consider a career as a professional artist.[1] Smit also attended the Teachers College of Columbia University.

After moving to New York City, Smit began studying with well-known printmaker Clare Romano. Although she had not done any printmaking previously, Smit appreciated the flexibility and the expressive possibilities of the medium. Inspired by Romano's career as both a professional artist and mother of two children, Smit also embraced printmaking as a mode of artistic expression that would allow her to balance motherhood and her burgeoning artistic career.

In 1972 Smit held her first individual exhibition at the Bratton Gallery in Greenwich Village where she showed *Harlem Games*, her first color woodcut. *Harlem Games* depicts five children playing double-dutch on a city sidewalk. The staccato rhythm of the jumpers is heightened by the energized white lines delineating the building's brickwork. The Hewitts, then clients of the gallery, bought this print from the exhibition. While not part of a series, *Harlem Games* is one of several prints focusing on children, including a self-portrait of the artist pregnant with her son Peter, titled *Peter's Mother*, and *King of the Hill*, also concerned with playing children.[2] Smit found, however, that her large-scale color woodcuts were more conducive to land-scapes such as *Woods City Magnified* (1980). She continued to explore the medium of color woodcut until 1976, when she began to experiment with lithography and intaglio while studying with William Maxwell at the

Teachers College. Subsequently, she incorporated a variety of complex print methods in her work.

Smit has traveled extensively throughout the Caribbean, South America, and Asia. Travel inspires her works, and the Caribbean has been a recurring theme for the last decade. A series titled *Sun People, Places and Things* was directly inspired by Barbados, where Smit has a home. These mixed-media works brim with the pastel colors of the Caribbean and capture the sun-drenched ambience of this spectacular setting.

Since 1996 Smit has been working on monotypes and mixed-media works, which focus on the Diaspora and her own family history. Smit employs personally significant objects and photographs overlaid by visual signs and symbols evocative of shamanistic vision. A current series focuses on chairs which both act as universal signifiers of presence/absence and evoke child-hood memories. Smit finds the series format liberating because she is free to vary the theme within a predetermined context. Printmaking continues to hold an allure for Smit. She is pleased that her works on paper are within reach of a range of collectors, because she is committed to others enjoying her work. Her monotypes also combine a more painterly technique with the rigors and rewards of printmaking.[3]

Smit has had twelve individual exhibitions, including *Sun Spaces* at the Barbados Museum and Historical Society, *Ten Years of Inspiration* at the James E. Lewis Museum at Morgan State University in Baltimore, Maryland, and *Sun People, Places and Things* at Viridian Gallery. Among the dozens of group shows in which Smit has participated are *The National Black Fine Art Show* in New York City, the *First Annual Alumni Exhibition* at the University of Pennsylvania, and *Artists Choose Artists* at the Viridian. Smit has curated two exhibitions: *Small Works* at the John Jay College of Criminal Justice in New York, and *Printmaking: The Process* at Cinque Gallery, in which she also participated.

William Maxwell's *Printmaking: A Beginning Handbook* (1977) featured Smit, and her work was included in *African-American Women Artists 1993*. Her essay titled "What is a Print" appeared in the catalogue for the exhibition *Art in Print: A Tribute to Robert Blackburn* at the New York Public Library. Smit's work is included in private and corporate collections, such as American Express Publications, Colgate-Palmolive, General Foods, the James E. Lewis Museum in Baltimore, the Federation of United Black Artists Collection in Johannesburg, South Africa, and the New York Public Library.

Pamela Kachurin

Ann Tanksley

Canal Builders II, 1989
oil on linen

New Wave, 1987
monotype

Ann Tanksley was born in Pittsburgh, Pennsylvania, in 1934. Although she first exhibited in the late sixties, she gained major recognition with work executed in the eighties and nineties. She has a voracious eye for forms and styles and has drawn upon the art of France and the Caribbean, as well as the work of African-American artists. Although she is best known for her imagistic response to the writings of Zora Neale Hurston, the three works in the Hewitt Collection demonstrate her ongoing search for new sources of inspiration.

Tanksley's growing popular acclaim derives, at least in part, from the immediacy of her work. The two paintings in the collection resulted from her visits to both Africa and the Caribbean: she painted figurative paintings in which the subjects are distinguished by saturated colors, clear outlines, and universality rather than specificity.[1] Her graphic style, which incorporates flat areas of intense color demarcated by either line or color contrasts, has prompted comparisons with Paul Gauguin and Henri Matisse.[2] Tanksley's paintings are more loosely painted than they first appear, an approach that adds vigor to the compositions.

Harvest of Shame (1979) depicts a row of migrant workers progressing on their hands and knees along a row. Tanksley celebrates labor while acknowledging the human cost: "The resilience of the human spirit and the ability of plants and vegetation to regenerate and grow after a horrendous spanking leaves hope that with the proper care and attention life will go on."[3] Her play with perspective, including the picture plane tilted into the viewer's space, intensifies both the composition and the content, while the strong diagonal creating at the conjunction of green foliage and red earth emphasizes the row of female workers. Garments, rather than physiognomy, distinguish one from the other. This painting conveys her concern for migrant workers and their relationship to a slave culture.[4] According to the artist, human and nature are enmeshed and to do right by one we must do right by the other.[5]

Canal Builders II (1989) combines unity and movement. The subject matter derived not only from her enduring interest in black workers, but also from her conversations with her cousin who had worked on the Panama Canal.[6] Like *Harvest of Shame*, this work uses color, line, and perspective to create a dramatic image that underscores content. Identically dressed in dark trousers, white shirts, and hats, the figures move in a boldly colored land-scape. Although reflective of her interest in black labor, both paintings in the Hewitt Collection move from the specific to the universal.

New Wave (1987), a monotype collage depicting a bust in profile, explores abstraction to a greater degree than did *Harvest of Shame* and *Canal Builders II*. Tanksley has described the piece as a self-portrait—one of only a few in her oeuvre—and as an exploration of the interplay between graphics and painting. According to Tanksley, she "need[s] both [media], to help [her] with composition and free form."[7]

Although Tanksley has produced art continuously, her children's departure from home has enabled her to immerse herself in her work. Says the artist: "My work is really very therapeutic to me. Now, I do it every day and in every way."[8] Growing public acclaim has led to a number of corporate com-missions. She was included in the popular *Absolut Vodka* series. Pepsico incorporated a work into an advertising campaign in 1995 and 1996. Coors Brewing Company selected *Brothers* for an advertising campaign commem-orating Martin Luther King, Jr. and *Canal Builders* for an advertisement cel-ebrating Black History Month. Such commissions have introduced her work to a broader, and highly appreciative, audience.

Kirstin Ringelberg

Harvest of Shame, 1979
oil on composition board

Henry O. Tanner

Seated Figure, ca. 1900
pencil on paper

The acquisition of Henry O. Tanner's landscape painting *Sand Dunes at Sunset, Atlantic City* for the Green Room of the White House in 1996—the first work by an African-American in that art collection—came nearly a century after the French government purchased *The Resurrection of Lazarus* for the Musée Luxembourg in 1897.[1] These events highlight the duality that existed in Tanner's life and art, both of which were shaped by two cultures on two continents. They are also a testament to the heights of critical acclaim that this Pittsburgh-native-turned-expatriate reached during his lifetime and during the fifty years following his death in his Paris apartment in 1937.[2]

Tanner's accomplishments were numerous.[3] He received an honorable mention for his first entry in the prestigious Paris Salon in 1895. Silver medals were awarded to his 1895 version of *Daniel in the Lion's Den* at the Universal Exposition in Paris in 1900 and the Pan-American exhibition in Buffalo in 1901. The status of *hors concours*, which allowed him to enter Salon exhibitions without being juried, was conferred upon the artist in 1906 along with a second place medal for *The Disciples at Emmaus*. The award Tanner considered to be his greatest achievement, chevalier de la Légion d'honneur, was bestowed upon him by the French government in 1923. In the United States, Tanner distinguished himself as the first African-American painter to teach at a black college and the first to be elected to the National Academy of Design.

Tanner's road to fame was also paved with failures and financial difficulties. Well into his adult years, Tanner depended upon his father, Benjamin Tanner—a bishop in the African Methodist Episcopal Church (A.M.E.) in Philadelphia, Pennsylvania—for the financial assistance he needed to pursue a career in art.[4] Between 1879 and 1885, he studied sporadically with Thomas Eakins at the Pennsylvania Academy of the Fine Arts where, in spite of the personal interest Eakins took in his work, Tanner suffered humiliating incidents of racial prejudice at the hands of the students.[5] In a bid for financial independence, Tanner established a portrait photography studio in Atlanta. The modest living he hoped to earn from photography in order to sustain his painting career failed to materialize. When the studio venture failed, he secured a teaching position at Clark University in Atlanta through contacts with A.M.E. Bishop and Mrs. Joseph C. Hartzell. The Hartzells, eager to support his study abroad, also arranged an individual show for the artist in Cincinnati, Ohio. When no sales were forthcoming, the Hartzells purchased the entire body of work for $300. Tanner used this money to set sail for Europe.

Tanner settled in Paris where he found a level of personal and professional acceptance that had eluded him in the United States. Following his studies at the Académie Julian with Jean-Joseph Benjamin Constant and Jean Paul Laurens, he traveled, painted, studied works of art in museum collections, found new patronage, and exhibited work. Living overseas precipitated a change in his artistic identity. In the United States he was viewed as an expatriate absorbed into French culture while abroad he was simply an American.[6] Although paradoxical, these dual identities afforded Tanner some measure of freedom outside the social constraints typically placed on the "Negro artist" working in the United States.[7] His marriage to Jessie MacCauley Olssen, a young opera singer of Swedish-Scottish descent from San Francisco, and the birth of their son, Jesse Ossawa Tanner in 1903, assured Tanner's continued expatriation due to the racial attitudes that prevailed at home.[8]

After his marriage in 1899, Tanner moved into a new studio on boulevard St. Jacques in Paris and devoted himself to painting. Newspaper reporters and writers for magazines such as *Cosmopolitan*, *Ladies' Home Journal*, *Brush and Pencil*, *Washington Colored American*, and *Harper's Weekly* sought out Tanner for interviews. His escalating international reputation also attracted African-American artists and tourists to his studio. Hale Woodruff, William E. Scott, and Palmer Hayden were among the younger generation of artists who admired Tanner and wanted to meet the reclusive artist during their travels abroad.[9] On the occasion of Woodruff's 1927 visit with Tanner

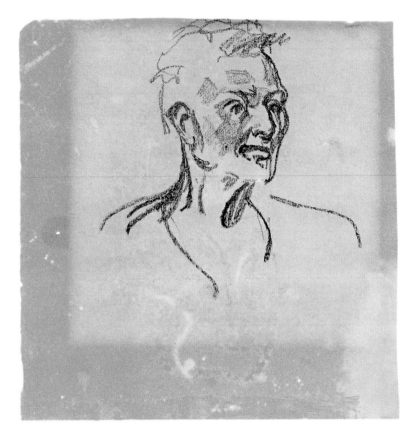

Head of a Man, recto, ca. 1900

pencil on paper

Head of a Man, verso, ca. 1900

pencil on paper

Gate in Tangiers, ca. 1910
oil on canvas

at Trépied near Étaples, the artist confessed that he had moved to this quiet Norman village to escape the constant interruptions he experienced in Paris.[10]

Although Tanner received the black artists who came to his door and maintained connections with the NAACP at home, the subjects he chose to paint made him vulnerable to attacks about his aloofness from the lives of African-Americans. Tanner's oeuvre included genre scenes related to French peasant life, vignettes of the First World War, landscapes, portraits, animal and marine subjects, and illustrations. But, his religious faith unquestionably provided the thematic foundation of his art. This prompted criticism from Alain Locke who felt Tanner had chosen to portray "Jewish Biblical types and subjects" instead of touching upon a mature "portrayal of the Negro subject."[11] But the majority of his contemporaries encouraged Tanner to work in the religious genre. Rodman Wanamaker, a Philadelphia merchant living in Paris, financed several of the artist's trips to the Holy Land to collect background material for his depictions of biblical themes. In the studio, Tanner developed compositions from studies of models—like the turbaned man depicted in the *Seated Figure*—and sketches of architectural views, as well as the photographs and postcards he gathered which served to stimulate his imagination and memory.[12]

Tanner first traveled to Algiers in 1908, drawn there by the orientalizing themes popularized in French art and literature. He returned to North Africa in 1912, this time to Tangiers, Morocco. Although undated, the oil painting titled *Gate in Tangiers* resembles the works described by Clara T. MacChesney when she visited his studio after his return from North Africa:

> His present style is much changed. Not only has he a greater breadth of vision, but his effects are cooler, grayer in tone and higher in key, not as black and brown in the shadows, or hot in color, as formerly. Thus his new canvases have a more spiritual, dreamlike quality. They are more poetical and show a great advance from earlier effects.[13]

The quality of light in North Africa fueled Tanner's consuming interest in enveloping the "total expression in a pervasive luminosity."[14] Tanner explained to the young Hale Woodruff what this meant:

> For myself, I see light chiefly as a means of achieving a luminosity, a luminosity not consisting of various light-colors but luminosity within a limited color range, say, a blue or blue-green. There should be a glow which indeed consumes the theme or subject. Still, a light-glow which rises and falls in intensity as it moves through the painting.[15]

The light depicted in *Gate in Tangiers* is brilliant, yet it evokes a tranquil mood and subdues the subject—figures seated against a massive, unadorned facade that recedes toward an equally austere gateway in the distance—without losing the sense of form and structure in the manner of impressionism.[16] A glowing luminance emerges through the keyhole gateway creating a dramatic counterpoint to the darker foreground. Tanner attained a Rembrandtesque balance of dark and light areas that favored expression over illustration.

The First World War unsettled Tanner, and his artistic production declined. Although his enthusiasm for making art returned after the war, he found that modernism had entered unfamiliar territories. The last decade of his life was marred by financial difficulties, the death of his beloved wife, Jessie, the illness of his son, and his own failing health. Nevertheless, the reputation Tanner had established at the turn of the century continued to sustain him. His work was included in exhibitions at home and abroad and in 1924, he held an individual exhibition at the Grand Central Art Galleries in New York. Today Tanner and his work have reached a new pinnacle of popularity owing to the complexity of his persona as a cosmopolitan expatriate painter and his enduring legacy as an inspirational figure for African-American artists.

Judy Bullington

Ellis Wilson

Haitian Camion, 1953
oil on composition board

Ellis Wilson was born in 1899 in Mayfield, Kentucky, a small town in the western-most part of the state surrounded by a patchwork of tobacco fields. The day-to-day activities of town and country people living there served as the subjects of sketches Wilson drew when he was not working odd jobs to help support the family or attending classes at the local segregated school.[1] His early artistic aspirations were influenced by his father, Frank Wilson, who had received minimal training from a white itinerant painter before settling into a career as a barber and cabinetmaker. Wilson recalled being inspired as a child by two of his father's oil paintings. One, a dark seascape, hung in the Wilson home and the other, a depiction of Christ driving the moneychangers from the Temple, was displayed in his father's Mayfield barbershop.[2]

Wilson left home with the intention of becoming an artist. Immediately after graduating from high school in 1917, he entered the Free State School for Black Students in Frankfort (now Kentucky State University) with the hope of studying art. Disheartened by the lack of art classes offered, Wilson persuaded his father to support a course of study in Chicago, Illinois, in the summer following the end of the First World War.[3] He enrolled in the Art Institute of Chicago and took night classes that focused on drawing from plaster casts. Wilson's academic training—studies of the nude model and still lifes in charcoal and oil—began in earnest in the fall of 1919. Students had free access to the galleries of the museum, an experience the artist equated with being in Paris.[4] Wilson flourished in this quasi-Parisian environment and upon graduation received both the George E. Hoe and Charles S. Peterson student prizes.

Wilson planned to stay in Chicago and work as a commercial artist but found that the predominately white studios were unwilling to deal directly with a black artist.[5] In 1928 he moved to New York and dedicated his creative efforts to fine art. He took private painting lessons from Xavier Barile while supporting himself with various types of daytime employment. The creative energy of the African-American communities of Harlem and downtown Manhattan during the 1930s and 1940s, and involvement with the Federal Art Project during those same decades, enabled Wilson to explore his artistic identity. Palmer Hayden, Alain Locke, Richmond Barthé, Alonzo Aden, and Joe and Beauford Delaney were among his

friends and acquaintances.[6] The academic techniques he learned at the Art Institute of Chicago were reshaped by a newfound appreciation for the bright angular work of Jacob Lawrence, the diversity of subject matter in Horace Pippin's scenes of black life, and the elongated forms of Aaron Douglas' silhouetted figures. Involvement with the Harlem Artists Guild, Artists Equity Association, and United American Artists, as well as participation in group exhibitions sponsored by the Harmon Foundation and the 1940 American Negro Exposition in Chicago garnered Wilson a modest reputation. He completed a series of triptych altarpieces for the Citizens Committee of the Army and Navy and did illustrations for the NAACP journal *The Crisis*. His first individual show was held at the Vendome Gallery in Manhattan in 1934.

A turning point in his career came in 1944 when Wilson was awarded a Guggenheim Fellowship, after four unsuccessful attempts. The scope of the project he proposed was broad—to conduct local studies of the Negro in the South, the West Indies, and Africa.[7] The project remained unfinished at the end of the year and in 1945 the fellowship was renewed. Monthly stipends from the foundation allowed Wilson to travel to Kentucky, Georgia, and the Carolinas. He sketched scenes from the lives of ordinary southern blacks, often focusing on the theme of labor, including workers in Kentucky clay mines, Georgia turpentine farms, and southern tobacco fields.[8] The paintings of Charleston street scenes and the fishing activities of the Geechee-speaking people who lived on Edisto and Beaufort islands off the coast of South Carolina and Georgia are the strongest reflection of Wilson's maturing style. Works from this series, such as *Charleston Flower Vendor*, place a modern face on a theme that had been popularized in the nineteenth century. Justus Bier, art critic for the *Louisville Courier-Journal* and Ellis Wilson's advocate, characterized these paintings as "poetical transcriptions eminently successful in transmitting the strong emotion attached to the subjects he chose to paint."[9]

Wilson avoided racially provocative themes instead choosing to depict blacks in the spirit of modern realism—wherever and however he observed them.[10] This was true of his paintings of the South as well as those completed between the early 1950s and his death in 1977. But the form of these later works shifted toward more colorful stylizations as a result of four trips to Haiti.[11] The money for his first trip came from the $3,000 second place prize his painting *Fisherwoman* won in the 1952 National Terry Art Exhibition.[12] During his two- or three-month stints in Haiti, Wilson immersed himself in the Caribbean experience by sketching vignettes and painting watercolor studies of the islanders and their traditions.[13] He then worked from memory, exaggerating local colors, altering poses, and accentuating the lithe silhouettes of the Haitians rather than details of expression or physiognomy. A quiet dignity distinguishes the featureless mourners portrayed in *Haitian Funeral Procession* and entangles the viewer in a scene veiled in unfamiliar trappings that evokes the ubiquitous experience of death.

The Contemporary Arts Gallery in New York showed Wilson's Haitian paintings in 1954. Works from this period ranged from frieze-like compositions of dancers and fishermen to rhythmic arrangements of beggars and street vendors.[14] Wilson's Haitian paintings seemed to give visual form to the Haitian scene as described by the dancer, cinematographer, and anthropologist Maya Deren in 1953:

> If a visitor to Haiti were to spend most of his time on a country roadside, he would have the sense of being a spectator at some theater-in-the-round, where a lyric dance drama of prodigious grace and infinite variety is in continuous performance…Even the groups of people—resting and talking in the high heat of mid-afternoon—seem to be "composed" in a painter's sense…[15]

It was not unusual for the artist to paint a second version of a popular scene with variations in color and subtle changes in design. According to Senta Bier, art editor of the *Louisville Courier-Journal*:

> [Wilson] twice painted a bus that brings farmers to the market in town, with locks of chickens crowded together on the roof of the bus. He painted this picture in two versions, one in the gayest reds, the other one in cooler colors, light blues and purples. It is interesting to observe in these two variants what colors mean to the painter.[16]

Haitian Camion (1953), which was purchased from the artist in 1973 by the Hewitts, depicts a red bus with Bel-Amour printed on the side. A man adjusts the luggage at the rear of the bus. Five women, two of whom balance baskets on their heads, have embarked from the still-crowded bus. This spectacle must have seemed curiously familiar to the artist whose childhood recollections included country people riding on buckboards and congregating at the swapping rings in Mayfield where the whites and blacks brought their animals on Saturdays and every third Monday.[17]

Wilson traveled with the Haitian artist Milo Pierre Antoine and befriended Pierre Monosiet, who would become the curator of the Haitian Art Museum in 1972, but his trips to the Caribbean ended when the political climate changed under Francois Duvalier. For the remainder of his career, Wilson painted in New York, preferring to sell his work privately to collectors rather than seeking the honor of individual shows. He died on 1 January 1977 in New York, having left his mark on the history of African-American art in the form of a perceptive documentation of his people in diverse cultural settings.[18]

Judy Bullington

Frank Wimberley

Seventy-Eight, 1978
collage

Although Frank Wimberley's nonrepresentational works are grounded in both abstract expressionism and European modernism, they also reflect his emotional and intellectual experience and serve as a testament to his artistic process. Born in 1926 in Pleasantville, New Jersey, Wimberley studied fine arts at Howard University, Washington, D.C., with Lois Mailou Jones, James Porter, and James Wells. Wimberley is quick to point out that while he learned painting techniques and discipline from his teachers, his true learning process began when he started to paint on his own. As a young man Wimberley saw the work of the abstract expressionists, admired their methods, and aspired to their accomplishments. Especially influential were the paintings of Jackson Pollock and Stuart Davis, which combined energetic abstraction with formal structure. Ultimately, however, Wimberley believes that an artist's vision determines his style, rather than the examples set by others.

While Wimberley occasionally deals with political subjects in his work, his "heart [is] in music." Wimberley, who had been a professional musician, continues to exploit the "unscheduled and unplanned" nature of jazz in his work.[1] Jazz is implicit in the improvisational nature of his approach and explicit in such works as *Sphere*, which alludes to Thelonious Monk. A trumpet player himself, Wimberley befriended Miles Davis and is continually inspired by his music, as well as that of Charlie Parker and Coleman Hawkins.[2] As Wimberley stated recently:

> The voice of jazz is the thread that runs through here. Spontaneous compositions and structures of varied moods and time signatures, exhibiting love and pain…These paintings are…derived from the music within.[3]

Seventy-Eight, a collage from 1978, incorporates newspapers, labels, and colored paper that retain letters whose placement evokes improvisation. Similar forms and shapes in different media accentuate both similarity and difference, like playing a tune in different keys. Wimberley employs acrylic in his painterly collages both as a binding agent and as an expressive medium. Bits of cardboard, found objects, and folded paper remain recogniz-

able three-dimensional forms, creating tension between tangible presence and pictorial illusion.

For Wimberley, abstraction, like a fingerprint, is unique to its creator. His works defy narrative and encourage each viewer to interpret the work in his or her own manner.[4] Titles are evocative rather than explicit, eliciting associations rather than imposing narrative. Although abstraction gives Wimberley the freedom to explore a variety of forms and modes of expression, he tempers this freedom with balance and structure. He fosters the unexpected and his own poetic descriptions reveal surprises imbedded in the works. While Wimberley acknowledges that because abstraction has "far fewer guarantees" than realism or photography, it generates excitement and interest. Developing a feeling from its first formulation to its "own particular conclusion is both the meaning and the process behind abstraction."[5]

Although he has established a successful career as an artist, Wimberley continually challenges himself and considers each new work as an opportunity to learn. Currently Wimberley is working on larger canvases (approximately five by five feet) which incorporate more unconventional textures such as sand and sawdust, which he says enliven the surfaces. The scale of these canvases at first intimidated Wimberley, but he has learned to enjoy the freedom and discipline it requires. Acrylic forces him to work quickly, decreasing the time between the act of painting and "seeing into the future of the painting."[6] His more recent works consider mass and void, achieving balance through contrast rather than color.

Wimberley makes his home in Sag Harbor, New York. He enjoys working and showing in the Hamptons because he is warmly received and he likes cultivating relationships with friends and patrons in that small community. Wimberley has mounted several individual exhibitions recently including *Recent Paintings* at the Bomani Gallery, San Francisco, the Cinque Gallery, and the June Kelly Gallery, New York. Other individual exhibitions include *Paintings, Collages and Wood Constructions* at Gallery Authentique in Roslyn,

New York, *Abstract Paintings* at Long Island University, and *An Alternative Perspective* at the Langston Hughes Cultural Center, New York. Wimberley has participated in numerous group exhibitions including *Eighteen Suffolk Artists* at the State University of New York at Stony Brook, *A Matter of Synthesis: Collage and Assemblage* at Arlene Bujese Gallery, East Hampton, New York, and group shows at the Museum of Modern Art, the Nassau County Museum of Art, the Albright-Knox Art Gallery, the Baltimore Museum of Art, and the Studio Museum in Harlem. His work is included in both corporate and museum collections such as Time Warner, Pepsico, the Metropolitan Museum of Art, and the Art Institute of Chicago.

Pamela Kachurin

Hale A. Woodruff

Country Church, 1935
linocut

Sentinel Gate, 1977

oil on canvas

After the Harmon Foundation awarded him a bronze medal and $100 for his landscape paintings in 1926, Hale A. Woodruff left for Paris, the cosmopolitan center of the art world.[1] In Paris, he departed from the more conservative style of painting he had learned at the Herron Art Institute in Indianapolis, Indiana, and at the Art Institute of Chicago. His painting, *The Card Players* (1928-29), instead drew inspiration from the paintings of Paul Cézanne and Pablo Picasso. In *The Card Players*, two figures with long faces and almond-shaped eyes contemplate the cards on the upwardly tilted table before them. Behind the figure on the left is a checkerboard floating in midair. At the lower right is a table supporting a leaning glass and a warped bottle. Bright reds, ochers, and blues compose its strange palette. The tilted perspective and shallow space emphasize the picture plane. The angular, elongated figures and masklike faces recall the African art that inspired Picasso's famous painting *Demoiselles d'Avignon* (1907), demonstrating Woodruff's willingness to employ the most modern art ideas.[2] Pictorial illusion, depth, perspective, naturalistic colors, and realistic figural representation have been abandoned in favor of the emphasis on composition and multiple viewpoints.

Several modern styles, including cubism, derived elements from non-Western art such as African sculpture which, up until the end of the nineteenth century, had ethnographic rather than artistic significance for many Europeans and Americans. African-American scholars noted the growing importance of African art in Europe. For example, Alain Locke's anthology *The New Negro*, which served as a philosophical guide for many artists of the Harlem Renaissance, discussed the importance of African forms for white artists and discouraged black artists from relying on such precedents. Instead, he insisted that they should create both a new art that was based on their own African heritage and an art criticism that suited these ends.[3] In fact, when Locke was in Paris, he and Woodruff became friends and both purchased African sculpture in the markets. As an art student in Indianapolis, Woodruff had been exposed to African art when a friend and supporter, Herman Leiber, gave the promising young artist Carl Einstein's

The Card Players, 1978

oil on canvas

book *Afrikanische Plastik*. Even though he could not read German, Woodruff studied its many photographs of African sculpture.[4]

The abstract styles in which Woodruff and many other American artists worked while in Europe remained unpopular in the United States, despite the introduction of European abstraction by both the Armory Show (1913) and the Museum of Modern Art in New York (founded in 1929). Woodruff, for example, questioned whether European abstraction was a suitable mode of expression in the United States, when Mexican artists had demonstrated that representational art could appeal to the masses.[5] American regionalists such as Thomas Hart Benton were creating an art that was not only realistic but also distinctly American.

Social protest also characterized some art and patronage during the 1930s. In 1935 the NAACP organized an exhibition titled *An Art Commentary on Lynching* that showed works by both black artists including Woodruff and white artists including Benton.[6] Held at the Arthur Newton Galleries in New York, it was among the rare interracial art exhibitions of the period. By contrast, although the Harmon Foundation-sponsored exhibitions promoted black artists otherwise excluded from the art establishment, some blacks perceived these events as segregationist.[7] Both social protest and regionalism informed Woodruff's print *Country Church* (1935). The undulating forms of the roof and the ragged clapboard siding show Benton's influence. Woodruff not only captured a region that was his home but also depicted social conditions without sentimentality or picturesqueness.[8]

In 1946 Woodruff received an appointment to New York University, where he savored the diverse postwar art scene. Woodruff drew and painted eroticized torsos, both male and female. At first glance, the torsos appear to be "[h]ighly abstract pieces...more studies of forms in space, studies of line, color and light than they are paintings which, like the gates or the murals, attempt to convey a specific concept or idea."[9] Using charcoal, Woodruff clearly defines large breasts, buttocks, and hips and models them in deep

shadow. These sensuous S-curved nudes resemble classical Greek sculptures of Aphrodite, the goddess of love. Woodruff appropriated the classical art canon, exaggerating and eroticizing it using an abstract formal vocabulary derived from contemporary abstraction and African sculpture.

In the fifties and sixties Woodruff's cryptic paintings assimilated the formal and symbolic language of African sculpture. Woodruff, who had an extensive library, was well acquainted with the meaning and context of African sculpture. In his *Celestial Gate* series, he combined and abstracted African art forms from different cultures such as Dogon granary doors (symbolizing the gate to heaven) bearing vertically arranged forms based on Asante geometric or figural gold weights (mnemonic devices referring to proverbs, some incorporated into African-American folklore).[10] Woodruff worked to develop a formal and symbolic hybrid that would speak to the sophistication and resonance of African-American culture and ancestry. *Sentinel Gate* (1977) exemplifies his strategy. The vertical arrangement of forms, the formal and chromatic isolation, and the appendagelike projections symbolize both sentinel and gate. Moreover, *sentinel* suggests a guardian or protective force perhaps reflecting the artist's preparation for death.[11]

David C. Hart

Two Torsos, ca. 1977

charcoal on paper

Notes

Understanding Celebration and Vision

1. Richard Powell, *Black Art and Culture in the 20th Century* (New York: Thames and Hudson, Ltd, 1997), 19.

2. Russell Ferguson, "Introduction: Invisible Center," in *Out There: Marginalization and Contemporary Culture*, ed. Russell Ferguson et al. (New York: The New Museum of Contemporary Art; Cambridge: The MIT Press, 1990), 13.

3. Cornel West, "The New Cultural Politics of Difference," in *Out There*, 27.

4. Ferguson, 9

5. Ibid., 11.

6. Michele Wallace, "Modernism, Postmodernism and the Problem of the Visual in Afro-American Culture," in *Out There*, 40.

7. bell hooks, *Art on My Mind* (New York: New Press, 1995), 2-3.

8. Stuart Hall, "What is this "Black" in Black Popular Culture?" in *Black Popular Culture*, ed. Gina Dent (Seattle: Bay Press, 1992), 30.

9. Powell, 22.

10. hooks, 3.

11. Ibid.

12. West, 28.

13. hooks, 2.

14. Hall, 25.

15. Ibid., 26.

Charles H. Alston

1. Romare Bearden and Harry Henderson, *A History of African-American Artists from 1792 to the Present* (New York: Pantheon Press, 1993), 261-262.

2. Ibid., 262.

3. Lizzetta LeFalle-Collins and Shifra M. Goldman, *In the Spirit of Resistance: African-American Modernists and the Mexican Muralist School* (New York: The American Federation of the Arts, 1996).

4. Lizzette LeFalle-Collins, "African-American Modernists and the Mexican Muralist School" in Lizzetta LeFalle-Collins and Shifra M. Goldman, *In the Spirit of Resistance: African-American Modernists and the Mexican Muralist School* (New York: The American Federation of the Arts, 1996), 34. *Man at the Crossroads* was later destroyed because of Rivera's inclusion of a portrait of Lenin in the work.

5. Sharon F. Patton, *African-American Art* (New York: Oxford University Press, 1998), 139-141.

6. Gylbert Coker, "Charles Alston: The Legacy," in *Charles Alston: Artist and Teacher* (New York: Kenkeleba Gallery, 1990), 10-11 and LeFalle-Collins, 1996, 34-35.

7. Gylbert Coker, "Art as History and Epic: The Murals," *Hale Woodruff: 50 Years of His Art* (New York: The Studio Museum in Harlem, 1979), 67-69.

8. Patton, 171.

9. Bearden and Henderson, 269

10. W.E.B. Du Bois, *The Souls of Black Folk* (1903; reprint, New York: Dover Publications, 1994), 2

John T. Biggers

1. Alvia J. Wardlow, *The Art of John Biggers: View From the Upper Room* (Houston: Museum of Fine Arts; New York: Harry N. Abrams, 1995), 16-18.

2. "The Web of Life: The Art of John Biggers," in ArtsEdNet (Malibu, CA: Getty Educational Institute for the Arts), available at //www.artsednet.getty.edu; Regenia A. Perry, *Free Within Ourselves: African-American Artists in the Collection of the National Museum of American Art* (Washington: National Museum of American Art, Smithsonian Institution; San Francisco: Pomegranate Artbooks, 1992), 37; Wardlow, 19. Lowenfeld, a Jewish refugee from Austria forced to leave because of Nazi persecution, knew all too well about racial prejudice.

3. Jeanne Zeidler, introduction to *The Art of John Biggers: View from the Upper Room* (Houston: Museum of Fine Arts; New York: Harry N. Abrams, 1995), 10; Jeanne Zeidler, "John Biggers," in *St. James Guide to Black Artists*, ed. Thomas Riggs (Detroit: St. James Press; New York: Schomburg Center for Research in Black Culture, 1997), 51.

4. "The Web of Life."

5. Perry, 37-38.

6. Brochure (Tampa: Museum of African American Art, 1994), n.p.; Lucinda H. Gedeon, *Artists Select: Contemporary Perspectives by Afro-American Artists* (Tempe: University of Arizona, 1986), 10.

7. "The Web of Life"; Perry, 38.

8. Brochure on the "Ascension" and "Origins" Murals by John Biggers (Winston Salem, NC: Delta Fine Arts, c. 1989), n.p.; "The Web of Life."

9. Jan Lose, "An Artist Comes Home to Honors" (n.p., n.d.), Hewitt Archival Papers; Wardlow, 16-18.

10. Samella Lewis, *African American Art and Artists* (Berkeley: University of California Press, 1978), 140.

11. The two youths may refer to the Ibeji twins, who, Biggers explains, are symbolic of a family's good fortune in Nigeria. See "The Web of Life."

12. Zeidler, "John Biggers," 52.

13. "The Web of Life."

14. Maya Angelou, "Reflection," in *The Art of John Biggers: View From the Upper Room* (Houston: Museum of Fine Arts; New York: Abrams, 1995), 14-15. Mae Tate, "John Biggers: The Man and His Art," *International Review of African American Art* 7 (1987): 42-56.

Margaret Burroughs

1. "Margaret Taylor Burroughs," *Contemporary Black Biography*, vol. 9 (Detroit: Gale Research, 1995): 23.

2. The story of the Polish exhibition, recounted by Eugene Pieter Feldman in his book commemorating the twentieth anniversary of the DuSable Museum, may be apocryphal. See his, *The Birth and Building of the DuSable Museum* (Chicago: DuSable Museum Press, 1981), 33. Burroughs did exhibit at the Friendship House in Moscow in 1967, following a 1965 trip to the USSR.

3. Reprinted in Feldman, 10.

4. Burroughs was married to Bernard Goss from 1937 to 1946.

5. Audrey Edwards, "They Made It Happen," *Black Enterprise* (May 1980), 35.

6. Edwards, 35.

7. Remarks at a White House Reception on the occasion of the National Conference of Artists, 2 April 1980. *Weekly Compilation of Presidential Documents* 16, 14 (7 April 1980), 600-603.

8. *Margaret Burroughs / Marion Perkins, A Retrospective* (Washington, D.C.: The Evans-Tibbs Collection, 1982); David Driskell, "Ten Elders at the Corcoran," *New Art Examiner* (June 1980), 8-21.

9. Quoted in *Forever Free: Art by African-American Women, 1862-1980*, curated by Jacqueline Fonvielle-Bontemps, published in conjunction with the exhibition of the same name (Alexandria, Virginia: Stephenson, Incorporated, 1980), 64.

Elizabeth Catlett

1. Elizabeth Catlett, "Responding to Cultural Hunger," in *Reimaging America: The Arts of Social Change*, eds. Mark O'Brien and Craig Little (Philadelphia: New Society, 1990), 244.

Ernest Crichlow

1. Barbara Lewis, *Ernest Crichlow*, unpublished paper, n.d., 4, Hewitt Archival Papers.

2. Ibid.

3. Mel Edwards, *Ernest Crichlow*, "An Afternoon with Ernest Crichlow," 4, Hewitt Archival Papers.

4. Lewis, 3.

5. Romare Bearden and Harry Henderson, *A History of African American Artist, from 1792 to the Present* (New York: Pantheon Books, 1993), 131.

6. Ernest Crichlow, telephone conversation with author, 28 September 1998.

7. Lewis, 3.

8. Crichlow, telephone conversation.

James Denmark

1. John Canaday, "Art—Two Rewarding Collage Shows," *New York Times*, 1 December 1973.

2. James Denmark, conversation with author, 30 September 1998.

Jonathan Green

1. Pat Conroy, foreword to *Gullah Images: The Art of Jonathan Green* (Charleston: South Carolina University Press, 1996), 7.

2. Rick Compton, "Artist Jonathan Green Puts the Community on Canvas," *The Naples Daily News*, 4 November 1993, 31.

3 Avery Chenoweth, "A Low Country Artist's Gullah Roots," *Beaufort* 2, 4 (Winter 1994): 50.

4. Jonathan Green, telephone conversation with author, 30 September 1998.

5. Ronne Hartfield, "Gathering Light in the Gray City. The Chicago Years," in *Gullah Images*, 23-8.

6. Lynn Robertson, "Walking with His Peers. The African American Artist in the South," in *Gullah Images*, 18-19.

J. Eugene Grigsby

1. Woodruff brought the most sophisticated of contemporary art studies to his students at both Morehouse and New York University; he studied at Harvard University, The Art Institute of Chicago, several academies in Paris, and with mural painter Diego Rivera. His work often dealt with African-American experiences; by the 1940s and 1950s, when Grigsby studied with him, Woodruff was associated with the abstract expressionists. Grigsby, Vivian Hewitt's cousin, introduced the collectors to Woodruff in New York, 1952. Regenia Perry, *Free Within Ourselves* (Washington, DC: National Museum of American Art; San Francisco: Pomegranate Artbooks, 1992), 183.

2. Eugene Grigsby, *Encounters: An Exhibit in Celebration of the Charlotte-Mecklenburg Bicentennial* (Charlotte, NC: Johnson C. Smith University; Phoenix, AZ: W. A. Krueger, 1968), 22. Most of the artists Grigsby included in the show had lived in the Charlotte area "at one time but for one reason or another moved to other communities" (2). The artists he exhibited are among the most celebrated today including Charles Alston, Romare Bearden, John Biggers, Ernest Crichlow, Sam Gilliam, Robert Gwathmey, Jacob Lawrence, Henry O. Tanner, Woodruff, among others.

3. Eugene Grigsby, "Celebrations of Peoples," *Celebrations of Peoples* (Honolulu: National Art Education Association Regional Conference Bulletin, 1972), 2.

4. Eugene Grigsby, telephone conversation with author, 13 September 1998.

5. Paul Von Blum, "Eugene Grigsby," in *St. James Guide to Black Artists*, ed. Thomas Riggs (Detroit: St. James Press; New York: Schomburg Center for Research in Black Culture, 1997), 222-3.

6. Eugene Grigsby, "Artists Statement," *Artists Select: Contemporary Perspectives by Afro-American Artists* (Tempe: Arizona State University, 1986), 14.

7. Von Blum, 222-3.

8. Grigsby, telephone conversation.

9. Grigsby, "Celebrations of Peoples," 2.

Earl Hill

1. Sharon F. Patton, *African-American Art* (Oxford and New York: Oxford University Press, 1998), 210.

2. Fern Hill, telephone conversation with author, 29 October 1998.

3. Helen A. Harrison, "Black Heritage Celebrated in Show," *New York Times*, 23 February 1986, 11.

4. Sharon F. Patton, *Memory and Metaphor: The Art of Romare Bearden* (New York: The Studio Museum in Harlem, 1991), 30.

Alvin C. Hollingsworth

1. Hollingsworth's birthdate also has been listed as 1931.

2. Hollingsworth created and syndicated the *Scorchy Smith* comic strip during the 1950s. "Alvin (C.) Hollingsworth," *St. James Guide to Black Artists*, ed. Thomas Riggs (Detroit: St. James Press, 1997); John H. Hewitt, "The Themes of Alvin C. Hollingsworth," *Black Art Quarterly* 2 (Fall 1977): 15.

3. Hewitt, 16.

4. *Pamphlet for Women*, an exhibition at Harbor Gallery, Cold Spring Harbor, New York, 1978. The artist published an article on women artists in 1979. A. C. Hollingsworth, "16 Women in the Art World," *National Scene Magazine Supplement* 7, 6 (August 1979): 12-14.

5. Quoted in Hewitt, 8. *Pamphlet for Women*, (Cold Spring Harbor, New York: Harbor Gallery, 1978), n.p.

6. Hewitt, 8.

7. Jeanne Siegel, "Why Spiral?" *Art News* 65 (September 1966): 48-51, 67-68; A. C. Hollingsworth and Mel Tapley, "Black Art Explosion," *National Scene Magazine Supplement* 6, 1 (June 1978): 4-6; Romare Bearden and Harry Henderson, *A History of African-American Artists from 1792 to the Present* (New York: Pantheon Books, 1993), 400-403.

8. Brochure on *Prophet Series* (Cold Springs Harbor, New York: Harbor Gallery, 1970), n.p.

9. Elsa Honig Fine, *The Afro-American Artist: A Search for Identity* (New York: Hacker Art Books, 1982), 247-249. Carolyn Margolis groups Hollingsworth with artists "who find their inspiration in the black protest movement, the black experience in America, or the motives, symbols, and color of Africa but work within an established tradition" (*The Barnett-Aden Collection* [Washington: Smithsonian Institution Press, published for the Anacostia Neighborhood Museum in cooperation with the Barnett-Aden Gallery, 1974], 21).

10. Judith E. Stein, "Figuring Out the Fifties: Aspects of Figuration in New York, 1950-1964," in *The Figurative Fifties: New York Figurative Expressionism* (Newport Beach, California: Newport Harbor Museum, 1988).

11. Mel Tapley, "Kwanzaa Artist-Renaissance Man," *National Scene Magazine Supplement* 7, 9 (December 1979): 9.

12. Barbara Haskell, "The Aesthetics of Junk," in *Blam! The Explosion of Pop, Minimalism, and Performance, 1958-1964* (New York: Whitney Museum of American Art in association with W. W. Norton & Co., 1984).

13. Quoted in Marshall Fishwick, "Contemporary Black Artists," commentary accompanying slides for *30 Contemporary Black Artists* at the Minneapolis Institute of Arts, October 17-November 24, 1968, quoted in Elsa Honig Fine, *The Afro-American Artist: A Search for Identity* (New York: Hacker Art Books, 1982), 247.

Ronald Joseph

1. "Negro Boy Artist Aims to Equal Whites," *Chicago Evening Post Magazine of the Art World*, 18 June 1929, clipping from the artist's file, Hewitt Archival Papers. The most complete account of the artist's youth and training is Ann Gibson's 1988 interview with the artist published in *Artist and Influence* 8 (1989), 58-73.

2. For an overview of the Harlem Renaissance and the role of black artists in the WPA, see "Emergence of African-American Artists During the Depression," in Romare Bearden and Harry Henderson, *A History of African-American Artists from 1792 to the Present* (New York: Pantheon Books, 1993), 227-344.

3. The Exposition, described by the *Chicago Daily Tribune* as "a Negro world's fair…celebrating 75 years of progress since emancipation," included 300 paintings and sculptures by African-American artists, as well as dioramas and murals. "Negroes Display Achievements in 1st World Fair," *Chicago Daily Tribune*, 5 July 1940, 9.

4. Ann Gibson discusses race, gender and the abstract expressionist canon in *Abstract Expressionism: Other Politics* (New Haven: Yale University Press, 1997).

5. *Modern Negro Art*, with a new preface by the author (1943; reprint, New York: Arno Press and the *New York Times*, 1969), 130.

6. The artist's remarks derive from an author interview and are published in "Ronald Joseph," in Bearden and Henderson, 398.

7. Ibid.

Jacob Lawrence

1. Ellen Harkins Wheat, *Jacob Lawrence: American Painter* (Seattle: Seattle Art Museum, 1986), 30.

2. Avis Berman, "Commitment on Canvas," *Modern Maturity* (August-September 1986): 72.

3. Michael Kimmelman, "An Invigorating Homecoming," *New York Times*, 12 April 1996, C4.

4. Berman, 74.

5. Kimmelman, C4.

6. The title of No. 7 reads: "Harriet Tubman worked as a water girl to cotton pickers; she also worked at plowing, carting and hauling logs." The work is in the *Harriet Tubman* series at Hampton University Museum, Hampton, Virginia.

Hughie Lee-Smith

1. Although many sources date Lee-Smith's birth to 1914, Lee-Smith's wife Patricia confirms 1915 as the correct date.

2. Carol Wald, "The Metaphysical World of Hughie Lee-Smith," *American Artist* (October 1978): 51.

3. "Two Afro-American Artists in an interview with Jay Jacobs," *Art Gallery* (April 1968): 29-30.

4. Wald, 51.

5. Reba and Dave Williams, "Themes and Images," in *Alone in a Crowd: Prints of the 1930s-40s by African American Artists from the Collection of Reba and Dave Williams* (Washburn Press, 1992), 33.

6. Vivien Raynor, "A Painter Finally Gets His Due," The *New York Times*, 4 December 1988.

7. Margot Mifflin, "Hughie Lee-Smith: 'It's a Topsy-Turvy World, Isn't It?'" *Art News* (October 1994): 89-90.

8. Mifflin, 89.

9. Mifflin, 90.

10. Vivian Hewitt, telephone conversation with author, 12 October 1998.

Virginia Evans Smit

1. Virginia Evans Smit, telephone conversation with author, 17 September 1998.

2. Smit, telephone conversation.

3. Smit, telephone conversation.

Ann Tanksley

1. Tanksley refers to her Caribbean and African travels as having directly affected the boldness of her colors in an interview with Donald Miller for the *Pittsburgh Post Gazette*, "Author and Black Life Spur Artist," 14 May 1992. Hewitt Archival Papers.

2. Helen A. Harrison, "Canny Landscapes and Other Scenes," *New York Times*, 24 December 1995.

3. Ann Tanksley, *Artist's Statement*, Analogies exhibition, SOHO 20, (New York, 1993).

4. Ann Tanksley, telephone conversation with author, 14 October 1998.

5. Tanksley, *Artist's Statement*

6. Tanksley, telephone conversation.

7. Ibid.

8. Ibid.

Henry O. Tanner

1. The French government purchased a second painting, *The Disciples at Emmaus*, for the same museum collection in 1906.

2. The increasing popularity of modern art after the turn of the century and the racial unrest of the 1960's had a negative impact upon the critical reception of Tanner's work. The revisionist scholarship of the 1970's and afterwards looked more favorably upon Tanner's work and his place in the history of art. Dewey F. Mosby, *Henry O. Tanner*, exh. cat. (Rizzoli: New York, Philadelphia Museum of Art, 1991), 16.

3. Tanner received some major form of recognition during every decade of his life from 1896 on. Mosby, 19.

4. Tanner's health was fragile. He fell ill in 1878 while apprenticing in a flour business to earn money for his art studies. This incident prompted Bishop Tanner to abandon the idea of his oldest son following him into the ministry and support his son's desire to pursue a career in art.

5. The printmaker Joseph Pennell was part of a group that symbolically "crucified" Tanner by binding him to his easel and leaving him in the middle of Broad Street. Pennell remarked that there had never been "a great Negro or Jew artist in the history of the world." Joseph Pennell, *The Adventures of an Illustrator, Mostly in Following his Authors in America & Europe* (Boston: Little, Brown and Co., 1925), 54.

6. Mosby, 15.

7. Tanner's expatriate status added another dimension to his public persona as an artist but it in no way suppressed discussions about his race. The issue of race as it related to the development of Tanner's art and career has been the focus of much scholarly debate. Dewey F. Mosby, *Across Continents and Cultures - The Art and Life of Henry Ossawa Tanner* (Kansas City, Missouri: The Nelson-Atkins Museum of Art, 1995), 7-9. Albert Boime, "Henry Ossawa Tanner's Subversion of Genre," *The Art Bulletin* 75 (September 1993): 415-442.

8. Regenia A. Perry, *Free Within Ourselves: African-American Artists in the Collection of the National Museum of American Art* (Washington, D.C.: National Museum of Art, Smithsonian Institution in association with Pomegranate Artbooks, San Francisco, 1992), 162.

9. Palmer Hayden described his contact with Tanner in a 1972 interview. James Adams, Camille Billops, James V. Hatch, "Palmer Hayden Painter," *Artist and Influence* 13 (1994): 91-105.

10. Hale A. Woodruff, "My Meeting with Henry O. Tanner," *The Crisis* 77 (Jan. 1970): 8.

11. Alain Locke, ed., *The New Negro* (1925; reprint, New York: Athenaeum, 1968), 265.

12. Tanner seldom worked with nude models in deference to his father's views about the sanctity of the human body. Mosby, "Across Continents and Cultures," 24.

13. Quoted in Mosby, "Henry Ossawa Tanner," 206.

14. Woodruff, 11.

15. Ibid.

16. While Tanner acknowledged Monet as one of the great painters of the day, he felt that the impressionist's efforts to capture atmospheric effects went too far in obscuring the sense of form and structure. Cézanne's innovations were more to his liking. Woodruff, 11.

Ellis Wilson

1. Wilson's first "public debut" as a budding artist came when he created an impromptu soap drawing on a dress shop window he had been hired to clean. The proprietor, pleased with the result, asked him to do more designs. See Justus Bier, "Ellis Wilson, Kentucky Negro Artist," *The Courier-Journal Magazine* (30 April 1950): 36.

2. Romare Bearden and Harry Henderson, *A History of African-American Artists From 1792 to the Present* (New York: Pantheon Books, 1993), 337.

3. Wilson did not enroll in a regular summer class right away because race riots broke out on State Street, near where the artist was staying, the day he arrived in Chicago. Camille Billops, "Ellis Wilson Visual Artist," *Artist and Influence* 13 (1994): 213-14.

4. Ibid., 214.

5. Ibid., 215.

6. Wilson felt a competitive hierarchy existed between the uptown artists in Harlem and the downtown artists living around East 18th Street where he eventually set up his studio. The uptown artists like Hale Woodruff, Charles "Spinky" Alston, Romare Bearden, Ernie Crichlow, and Norman Lewis were acquaintances. His friendships revolved around downtown artists including Palmer Hayden, Joe and Beauford Delaney, the illustrator Robert Pious, and the painter Johnny Atkinson. Billops, 220, 223.

7. Wilson won the Guggenheim Fellowship for his depiction of black defense plant workers. The documentation of southern blacks was intended to complete the story of migration of African Americans from southern farmlands to the war plants in the industrial north. Michael Carter, "Ellis Wilson, N.Y. Artist, Is Winner of Guggenheim Award," The Ellis Wilson Papers, The Archives of American Art (Microfilm Reel #3).

8. David P. Duckworth, "Ellis Wilson's Pursuit of a Theme on Labor," *International Review of African-American Art* 9, 4 (1990): 4-49.

9. Bier, 37.

10. He could not bring himself to participate in a WPA gallery show that centered on the theme of lynching. Billops, 224. Wilson was acknowledged as an "Interpreter of Negro Life." Rex Goreleigh, "Ellis Wilson," *Bronze Citizen* (June 1946): 24.

11. Wilson did not date his paintings which has generated conflicting information about the chronology of his work. Some sources have dated his Haitian paintings as early as 1940, but in the artist's 1975 interview with Camille Billops, he stated that he did not go to Haiti until after the Second World War. Billops, 221.

12. Dr. Justus Bier was among the jurors of the competition. Arthur Miller, "Terry's Big-Scale Business: A Bonanza in Miami," *Art Digest* 26 (1 March 1952): 10.

13. Billops, 222.

14. Eleanor C. Munro, "Reviews and Previews: Ellis Wilson," *Art News* 52 (Feb. 1954): 47, 58-59.

15. Maya Deren, "Divine Horsemen: The Living Gods of Haiti," quoted in Seldon Rodman, *Where Art is Joy Haitian Art: The First Forty Years* (New York: Ruggles de Latour, 1988), 161.

16. Senta Bier, "Art: Paintings by Ellis Wilson Shown In New York Gallery," *The Courier-Journal Louisville*, 14 February 1954.

17. Billops, 213.

18. A special note of gratitude is extended to Albert Sperath, Director of University Art Galleries at Murray State University in Kentucky, who so generously shared his expertise and material on Ellis Wilson. Mr. Sperath's forthcoming book on Ellis Wilson will be published by the University Press of Kentucky.

Frank Wimberley

1. Frank Wimberley, telephone conversation with author, 29 September 1998.

2. Rose Slivka, *Frank Wimberley: New Paintings* (New York: n.p., 1997), 4. Hewitt Archival Papers.

3. "Frank Wimberley Artist's Statement," *Collection Insights* (Islip, N.Y.: n.p., 1997). Hewitt Archival Papers.

4. Wimberley, phone conversation.

5. *Frank Wimberley: Recent Works* (New York: Alley Cat Gallery, 1993), 3.

6. Wimberley, phone conversation.

Hale A. Woodruff

1. Winifred Stoelting, "The Atlanta Years: A Biographical Sketch" in *Hale Woodruff: 50 Years of His Art* (New York: The Studio Museum in Harlem, 1979), 12.

2. Ibid., 30.

3. See Alain Locke, "The New Negro" and "Legacy of the Ancestral Arts" in *The New Negro: An Interpretation* (New York: Albert & Charles Boni, 1925). Most of the essays in this important anthology appeared in 1924 when editor Paul Kellogg published a special edition of the literary journal *Survey Graphic* titled *Harlem: Mecca of the New Negro* in response to the suggestion of W.E.B. Du Bois that black scholars and critics should take a greater role in the emerging "Harlem Renaissance." Sharon F. Patton, *African-American Art*. (Oxford and New York: Oxford University Press, 1998), 114-115.

4. Albert Murray, "An Interview with Hale Woodruff" in *Hale Woodruff: 50 Years of His Art* (New York: The Studio Museum in Harlem, 1979), 77-78.

5. Romare Bearden and Harry Henderson, *A History of African-American Artists from 1792 to the Present* (New York: Pantheon Press, 1993), 204-205.

6. Campbell, 1979, 32-33 and Harriet G. Warkel "Image and Identity: The Art of William E. Scott, John W. Hardrick, and Hale A. Woodruff," in William E. Taylor and Harriet G. Warkel, *A Shared Heritage: Art by Four African-Americans*, (Indianapolis: Indianapolis Museum of Art, 1996), 64.

7. For a critical assessment of the Harmon Foundation's exhibitions as well as the artists who participated in them, see Gary A. Reynolds and Beryl J. Wright, *Against the Odds: African-American Artists and the Harmon Foundation* (Newark: Newark Museum, 1989).

8. Campbell, 1979, 32.

9. Ibid., 57.

10. Ibid., 36, and Corrine Jennings, "Hale Woodruff: African-American Metaphor, Myth and Allegory" in *A Shared Heritage*, 84.

11. Jennings, 97.

Checklist for Hewitt Collection

(Dimensions given in inches; height precedes width)

Charles H. Alston (1907-1977)
Woman Washing Clothes, ca. 1970
Oil pastel on paper
30-1/2" x 20-1/2"

Romare Bearden (1912-1988)
Morning Ritual, 1986
Collage with acrylic on plywood
20" x 6-3/4"

Romare Bearden (1912-1988)
Harlem Street Scene, ca. 1973
Lithograph
30" x 24"

Romare Bearden (1912-1988)
Homage to Mary Lou, 1984
Lithograph
29" x 20"

Romare Bearden (1912-1988)
Jamming at the Savoy, ca. 1988
Lithograph
22" x 30"

John T. Biggers (1924-)
Family #1, 1974
Charcoal on paper
32" x 23"

John T. Biggers (1924-)
Family #2, 1975
Lithograph
26" x 20"

John T. Biggers (1924-)
Twins of Morning, 1975
Lithograph
26" x 20"

Margaret Burroughs (1917-)
Warsaw, 1965
Linocut
17" x 13-3/4"

Elizabeth Catlett (1915-)
Head of a Woman, 1967
Lithograph
19-5/8" x 14-1/2"

Ernest Crichlow (1914-)
Woman in a Blue Coat, ca. 1948
Oil on canvas
20" x 16"

Ernest Crichlow (1914-)
The Balcony, 1980
Collage and acrylic on paper
15" x 20"

Ernest Crichlow (1914-)
Boy in a Green Field, ca. 1979
Acrylic on composition board
31-1/2" x 21"

Ernest Crichlow (1914-)
Girl With Flowers, ca. 1979
Acrylic on composition board
31" x 21"

Ernest Crichlow (1914-)
Woman in a Yellow Dress, ca. 1980
Collage with tempera on paper
22" x 17"

Ernest Crichlow (1914-)
Suburban Woman, 1979
Collage with acrylic on paper
19-3/4" x 15"

Ernest Crichlow (1914-)
Waiting, ca. 1965
Lithograph
19-1/2" x 14"

Ernest Crichlow (1914-)
Ronnie, 1965
Lithograph
20" x 13"

Ernest Crichlow (1914-)
Street Princess, 1982
Serigraph
38-5/8" x 26-1/4"

Ernest Crichlow (1914-)
The Sisters, 1979
Serigraph
26-1/4" x 40"

James Denmark (1936-)
Daily Gossip, ca. 1975
Collage on panel
8-1/2" x 7"

James Denmark (1936-)
Two Generations, 1984
Lithograph
28" x 22"

James Denmark (1936-)
Untitled, ca. 1983
Watercolor
14" x 10"

James Denmark (1936-)
Head, 1973
Collage
20" x 14-1/4"

Jonathan Green (1955-)
Folding Sheets, 1989
Acrylic on canvas
20" x 15-3/4"

Jonathan Green (1955-)
Easter, 1989
Acrylic on paper
11-1/4" x 7-1/2"

Eugene J. Grigsby (1918-)
Black, Brown, and Beige, 1963
Oil on canvas
20" x 30-1/2"

Eugene J. Grigsby (1918-)
Abstraction in Red and Black, ca. 1963
Oil on canvas
26" x 34"

Eugene J. Grigsby (1918-)
Specters, 1970
Oil on canvas
17" x 22"

Eugene J. Grigsby (1918-)
African Journey: The Bridge, ca. 1981
Serigraph
22" x 30"

Eugene J. Grigsby (1918-)
The Enchantress, ca. 1979
Lithograph
20-1/4" x 15"

Eugene J. Grigsby (1918-)
No Vacancy, ca. 1979
Woodcut
21-3/4" x 16-1/2"

Eugene J. Grigsby (1918-)
Inner View, ca. 1978
Lithograph
26" x 19"

Earl Hill (1927-1985)
Weight of the World, 1967
Watercolor
9-1/2" x 5-3/4"

Earl Hill (1927-1985)
Beulah's World, 1968
Oil on composition board
24" x 30"

Earl Hill (1927-1985)
The Presence, 1974
Oil on wood
20" x 7"

Alvin C. Hollingsworth (1931-)
Tomorrow, ca. 1977
Oil and India ink on canvas board
15" x 12"

Alvin C. Hollingsworth (1931-)
African Village, ca. 1978
India ink and oil on canvas
13" x 17"

Alvin C. Hollingsworth (1931-)
Waiting #2, ca. 1977
Oil and acrylic collage
12" x 9"

Alvin C. Hollingsworth (1931-)
Family Tree, ca. 1977
Lithograph
26" x 22"

Ronald Joseph (1910-1992)
The Family, ca. 1953
Mixed media on paper
23-3/4" x 18-7/8"

Ronald Joseph (1910-1992)
Two Musicians, 1952-55
Lithograph
32" x 24"

Ronald Joseph (1910-1992)
Still Life, 1950-54
Mixed media on paper
17-1/2" x 22"

Jacob Lawrence (1917-)
Playing Records, 1949
India ink on paper
23" x 18"

Hughie Lee-Smith (1915-)
Signaler II, 1983
Oil on canvas
9" x 12"

Virginia Evans Smit (1936-)
Harlem Games, ca. 1964
Woodcut
20-1/2" x 18-1/2"

Ann Tanksley (1934-)
Harvest of Shame, 1979
Oil on composition board
24" x 18"

Ann Tanksley (1934-)
Canal Builders II, 1989
Oil on linen
36" x 25-1/2"

Ann Tanksley (1934-)
New Wave, 1987
Monotype
10-1/2" x 6"

Henry O. Tanner (1859-1937)
Seated Figure, ca. 1900
Pencil on paper
9-1/2" x 9-1/4"

Henry O. Tanner (1859-1937)
Head of a Man, recto, ca. 1900
Pencil on paper
9-1/4" x 8-3/4"

Henry O. Tanner (1859-1937)
Head of a Man, verso, ca. 1900
Pencil on paper
9-1/4" x 8-3/4"

Henry O. Tanner (1859-1937)
Gate in Tangiers, ca. 1910
Oil on canvas
18-1/4" x 15"

Ellis Wilson (1899-1977)
Haitian Camion, 1953
Oil on composition board
19-1/4" x 29"

Frank Wimberley (1926-)
Seventy-Eight, 1978
Collage
19-1/2" x 16"

Hale A. Woodruff (1900-1980)
The Card Players, 1978
Oil on canvas
36" x 42-1/4"

Hale A. Woodruff (1900-1980)
Sentinel Gate, 1977
Oil on canvas
40" x 30"

Hale A. Woodruff (1900-1980)
Two Torsos, ca. 1977
Charcoal on paper
27-3/4" x 20"

Hale A. Woodruff (1900-1980)
Country Church, 1935
Linocut
12" x 12-1/4"

List of Contributors

Lili Corbus Bezner
Currently an assistant professor of art history at University of North Carolina at Charlotte, Dr. Bezner specializes in American art of the twentieth century. Her book *Photography and Politics in Cold War America* is forthcoming from Johns Hopkins University Press. Dr. Bezner's research has been published in *History of Photography* and *The Southern Quarterly*.

Judy Bullington
Dr. Judy Bullington is an assistant professor of art history at Western Oregon University. Her specialties include American art at the turn of the century. She has held teaching position at Southwestern University and has received fellowships from institutions such as Winterthur. Her research has appeared in *Gazette des Beaux-Arts*.

Kristin U. Fedders
A doctoral candidate at the University of Pennsylvania, Ms. Fedders specializes in American and modern art and the history of modern design. She is currently a lecturer at Lake Forest College and at the School of the Art Institute of Chicago. She has published in *New Art Examiner*, *American Indian Art Magazine*, and exhibition catalogues. She has presented papers throughout the United States and Canada.

David C. Hart
A doctoral candidate in art history at the University of North Carolina at Chapel Hill, Mr. Hart specializes in the study of African-American art. Most recently, he has contributed to the forthcoming exhibition catalogue, *To Conserve a Legacy: American Art from Historically Black Colleges and Universities*. This project was organized by the Addison Gallery of Art and the Studio Museum of Harlem.

Herb Jackson
A professor of art at Davidson College, Herb Jackson is an internationally acclaimed painter. His works have been exhibited throughout the United States, the United Kingdom, South America, and Japan. His paintings are part of the permanent collection of institutions such as the Whitney Museum of American Art, the Brooklyn Museum of Art, the Smithsonian Institution, and the British Museum. He has received fellowships from the National Endowment for the Arts and the Southeastern Center for Contemporary Art. He was a student and friend of Romare Bearden.

Pamela Kachurin
At present a research associate at the Davis Center for Russian Research at Harvard University, Dr. Pamela Kachurin specializes in twentieth-century art. She has taught at Northeastern University, Tufts University and Endicott College and has presented papers throughout the United States and Canada.

Karen Kettering
A specialist in twentieth-century art, Dr. Karen Kettering is associate curator of Russian art at the Hillwood Museum in Washington, D.C. Prior to Hillwood, Dr. Kettering was assistant professor of art history at the University of Dayton. She has lectured throughout the United States and Europe on modern art and has held a fellowship at the Getty Center for Art.

Lizzetta LeFalle-Collins
Formerly curator of visual art at the California Afro-American Museum in Los Angeles, Dr. LeFalle-Collins has been an independent curator since 1992. Shows curated under her direction include *Sargent Johnson, African-American Modernist* and *In the Spirit of Resistance: African-American Modernists and the Mexican Muralists School*. She is also a contributor to the current Jacob Lawrence catalogue raisonne.

Regenia Perry
Professor emerita in African and African-American art history at Virginia Commonwealth University, Dr. Regenia Perry has been instrumental in the research in African-American art for over three decades. Her publications include *Free Within Ourselves: African American Art from the National Museum of American Art Collection* and *Harriet Power's Bible Quilt*. Dr. Perry has held teaching positions at Howard University and Harvard University and fellowships at the National Museum of American Art, Yale University, the Metropolitan Museum of Art, and the National Endowment for the Humanities.

Kirstin Ringelberg
Ms. Ringelberg is currently a doctoral candidate in art history at the University of North Carolina at Chapel Hill. She has served as an instructor in the department of art history at the university and has presented papers throughout the United States. Her current research interests include issues of domesticity in painted representations of artist's studios.

Todd D. Smith
Curator of American art at the Mint Museum, Mr. Smith specializes in American art and culture of the nineteenth and twentieth centuries. He has served as the curator of American art at the Dayton Art Institute and curator of collections at the Kinsey Institute for Research in Sex, Gender and Reproduction in Bloomington, Indiana. He has authored several exhibition catalogues and has published in *History of Photography*. In addition, he has presented papers throughout the United States and Great Britain.

Production Notes

Publication Design   RLR Associates, Inc. - Indianapolis, IN
Rodney Reid, *design director*
Muzio Lorusso, *graphic designer*
Deb Durham-Raley, *design editor*

Photography   David Ramsey - Charlotte NC (*unless otherwise noted*)

Prepress Production   Rheitone, Inc. - Indianapolis IN

Print Production   Classic Graphics - Charlotte NC

Specifications   Text Fonts: Filosofia, Dead History (Emigre)
Paper: Potlatch, Vintage (Gloss & Velvet)
Separations: 200 lines per inch
Print: Four-color process + one pms + spot varnish